lc

P

MIAMI

TOP SIGHTS · LOCAL EXPERIENCES

T0276705

ADAM KARLIN,
ANTHONY HAM

Contents

Plan Your Trip   4

Rooster sculpture, Little Havana
GORAN VRHOVAC/SHUTTERSTOCK©

Explore
Miami

Worth a Trip 🔭

Miami's Walking Tours 🥾

South Beach (p42) MARGARET.WIKTOR/SHUTTERSTOCK©

Wynwood & the Design District (p85)

A hotbed of creativity, with street murals, indie boutiques and buzzing nightlife. Known for art galleries and microbreweries.

North Beach (p55)

Home to less-touristy beaches and a mangrove-filled state park. The postwar architecture hides many options for nighttime.

Wynwood Walls
◉

Adrienne Arsht Center for the Performing Arts
◉
◉ *Pérez Art Museum Miami*
◉

◉ Art Deco Historic District

Bayfront Park

South Beach (p35)

Fabled destination for shoreline fun, nightlife and art-deco architecture, Miami Beach also has cultural sights and shopping.

Downtown Miami (p65)

Easily accessible area with beautiful museums, concert halls, waterfront green space, plus great drinks and dining.

Explore Miami 33

Worth a Trip

Survival Guide 147

Special Features

COVID-19

We have re-checked every business in this book before publication to ensure that it is still open after 2020's COVID-19 outbreak. However, the economic and social impacts of COVID-19 will continue to be felt long after the outbreak has been contained, and many businesses, services and events referenced in this guide may experience ongoing restrictions. Some businesses may be temporarily closed, have changed their opening hours and services, or require bookings; some unfortunately could have closed permanently. We suggest you check with venues before visiting for the latest information.

Welcome to Miami

Miami straddles the Caribbean, North America and Latin America like nowhere else on Earth and showcases its diversity via a constant assault of sensory pleasure. Art deco architecture and graffiti murals are the backdrop, Cuban coffee is the fuel, and reggaetón and clacking dominoes are the soundtrack to a city tinged by pink sunsets on a silver skyline and humid air whispering off Biscayne Bay.

Top Sights

Art Deco Historic District

America's most captivating art deco district. **p36**

ULLSTEIN BILD/GETTY IMAGES ©

Wynwood Walls

Miami's best collection of street art. **p86**

Pérez Art Museum Miami

Miami's epicenter of contemporary art, designed by Herzog & de Meuron. **p66**

Vizcaya Museum & Gardens

Fantastical palace on Biscayne Bay. **p116**

Adrienne Arsht Center for the Performing Arts

Miami's top performing arts hall. **p68**

Bayfront Park

Downtown Miami's waterfront park. **p70**

Fairchild Tropical Garden

South Florida's most beautiful gardens. **p128**

Cuban Memorial Boulevard Park

Shrine and living history. **p104**

Biltmore Hotel

Architectural beauty from the 1920s. **p130**

Everglades National Park

A tide-tossed wetland wonder. **p140**

Eating

Miami has tons of immigrants from every inhabited continent, and it's a sucker for food trends. Thus you get a good mix of cheap ethnic places to eat and high-quality top-end cuisine, alongside some poor-value dross in touristy zones. You can eat well anywhere here, from cutting-edge trendsetters Downtown to tiny Cuban cafes in Little Havana.

Cuban Cuisine

Cuban food mixes Caribbean, African and Latin American influences, and in Tampa and Miami it's a staple of everyday life. Sidle up to a Cuban *lonchería* (snack bar) and order a *pan cubano:* a buttered, grilled baguette stuffed with ham, roast pork, cheese, mustard and pickles (pictured). In the morning, try a Cuban coffee, also known as *café cubano* or *cortadito.* This hot shot of liquid gold is essentially sweetened espresso, while

café con leche is just café au lait with a different accent: equal parts coffee and hot milk.

Latin Influences

Thanks to an enormous influx of Caribbean, Central American, and Latin American immigrants, the Miami area offers first- and second-generation eateries from across the Western Hemisphere. Seek out Haitian *griots* (marinated fried pork), Jamaican jerk chicken, Brazilian barbecue, Central

American *gallo pinto* (red beans and rice) and Nicaraguan *tres leches* (three milks' cake).

Food Trucks

Food trucks are ubiquitous in Miami. For both immigrants and young natives, a food truck offers a business opportunity with considerably reduced overheads and financial risk. There are far too many trucks in town to list here, but if you want a taste of what's good on four wheels, there are plenty of places where food trucks

BONCHAN/SHUTTERSTOCK©

regularly gather, including the monthly Wynwood Art Walk (p22), the Wynwood Marketplace (p94) on any given evening, or Haulover Beach Park (p58) from 5pm to 9pm on Tuesdays.

Creative Restaurants

Kyu Innovative, flame-kissed cooking in Wynwood. (p95)

27 Restaurant In Mid-Beach, find a globally inspired menu and great atmosphere. (p58)

1 800 Lucky Diversity reigns at this Singapore-style food hall. (p96)

Vegetarian Options

Verde Gorgeous vegetarian fare in the Pérez Art Museum. (p79)

Last Carrot Coconut Grove mainstay with excellent vegetarian choices. (p123)

Kush Lots of vegetarian depth out in Wynwood. (p96)

Threefold Australian-style cafe in Coral Gables. (p136)

Affordable Eats

Puerto Sagua Down-home Cuban diner in South Beach. (p48)

Cake Thai Rich taste of Thailand, plunked down in Wynwood. (p98)

Coral Bagels Bagels are life; this spot makes great ones. (p122)

Wynwood Marketplace Food trucks, beer and live music. (p94)

Latin Cuisine

Doce Provisions Creative takes on Latin American classics. (p107)

Versailles Long-running Cuban institution near Little Havana. (p107)

El Nuevo Siglo Home-cooked flavors served in a supermarket. (p107)

Enriqueta's A standout, blue chip Puerto Rican diner. (p95)

Drinking & Nightlife

Miami has an intense variety of bars, ranging from grotty jazz and punk dives (with excellent music) to beautiful lounges, cocktail bars blended with tropical gardens and Cuban dance halls. Miami's nightlife reputation for being all about wealth, good looks and phoniness is thankfully mostly isolated to the South Beach scene.

Rooftop Bars

Miami's high rises are put to fine use by the many rooftop bars you'll find scattered around the city. These are usually located in high-end hotels found in Miami Beach and in Downtown. The view is, of course, the big reason to come – and it can be sublime, with the sweep of Biscayne Bay or a sparkling beachfront in the background. Despite being in hotels, some spots are a draw for locals and it can be quite a scene, with DJs, a dressy crowd and a discriminating door policy at prime time on weekend nights. If you're here for the view and not the party, come early. Happy hour is fabulous – you can catch a fine sunset and getting in is usually not a problem.

Microbreweries & Beer Bars

The Pacific Northwest gets a lot of beer attention, but the complete opposite corner of the American map is also a playground for craft brewers. At multiple Miami locales, you'll find creative brews and a strong neighborhood vibe. Some stock other beers on rotating taps (with a focus on South Florida brewers) as well as their own. Most microbreweries also have food available, or work with food trucks who park outside.

Wynwood is the epicenter of the beer scene, with a handful of brewers, plus beer-focused bars and eateries. With soaring real-estate prices in the neighborhood however, more brewers are choosing to open in other parts of the city. Most local gastropubs (popular

ALEXANDER SPATARI/GETTY IMAGES©

in Coral Gables) heavily emphasize local brews.

Best Atmosphere

Broken Shaker A garden of tropical allure (plus fine cocktails and pretty people). (p60)

Sweet Liberty Laid-back local crowd, friendly bar staff and great drinks. (p49)

The Anderson The perfect neighborhood bar on the Upper East Side. (p63)

Ball & Chain Always a good time at this Little Havana classic. (p109)

Baby Jane A slick, tropical-themed Downtown cocktail bar. (p82)

Best Neighborhood Bars

Lost Boy Great, casual-vibe Downtown bar in an old building. (p81)

Wood Tavern Where the Wynwood folks like to rub shoulders. (p99)

Bob's Your Uncle Easygoing bar in a nice corner of Mid-Beach. (p61)

Mama Tried Friendly joint for drinks and dancing Downtown. (p82)

Best Hidden Gems

Bodega Den of debauchery hidden behind a taco stand. (p49)

Vagabond Pool Bar Fancy, fresh hotel pool bar. (p63)

Blackbird Ordinary First-rate on all counts: cocktails, music, crowd. (p81)

The Corner Non-fussy, hip bar next to Downtown good times. (p81)

Best Dive Bars

Kill Your Idol A South Beach watering hole with soul. (p50)

Mac's Club Deuce A dingy, Miami Beach classic. (p49)

On The Rocks Where Mid-Beach goes for a friendly beer. (p61)

Shopping

Miami boasts plenty of high-end fashion, designer sunglasses, vintage clothing, books, records, Latin American crafts, artwork, gourmet goodies and more. While there are plenty of malls in Miami, new shopping centers are often built in the style of outdoor arcades or bazaars, allowing shoppers to enjoy the sunny weather.

The Lincoln Road Experience

Lincoln Road Mall (pictured above), an outdoor pedestrian thoroughfare between Alton Rd and Washington Ave in South Beach, is all about seeing and being seen; there are times when Lincoln feels less like a road and more like a runway. Carl Fisher, the father of Miami Beach, envisioned the road as a Fifth Ave of the South. Morris Lapidus, one of the founders of the loopy, neo-baroque Miami Beach style,

designed much of the mall, including shady overhangs, waterfall structures and traffic barriers that look like marbles a giant might play with.

Shopping Miami Beach

Other parts of Miami Beach hold their own shopping rewards. More high-end shoppers tend to skirt around South Beach and head north to Sunset Harbour, which has a few colorful boutiques (plus great coffee, pastries and restaurants nearby).

In the southern end of Collins Ave, below about 9th St, you'll find a mix of indie boutique and mid-range chains such as Steve Madden, Club Monaco and Banana Republic. One block over, Washington Ave is also dotted with stores (surf shops, liquor shops and footwear retailers like Vans). There's also shopping along Ocean Dr itself, though the offerings aren't great. It's mostly taken over by souvenir and T-shirt shops, with a few antique stores.

KAMIRA/SHUTTERSTOCK©

Wynwood & the Design District

On the mainland, there are several good shopping destinations. Wynwood has some of the most appealing collections of indie designers, galleries and crafty stores that sell unique items (handblown vases, beautifully made stationery, Detroit-made watches).

For high-end everything (clothing, accessories, artworks, baked goods), the neighboring Design District is the place to be. The main concentration of stores runs along palm-tree-lined 39th and 40th Sts.

Fashion & Accessories

Supply & Advise Downtown shop with ruggedly elegant menswear. (p83)

Havana Collection Good spot for *guayaberas* (Cuban dress shirts) and similar. (p111)

Boy Meets Girl Kids meet high fashion in Coral Gables. (p139)

Books

Books & Books Atmospheric spot for browsing, with a great cafe. (p53)

Taschen Tiny shop, big beautiful art books. (p53)

Gifts & Souvenirs

La Isla Little Havana shop with contemporary Cuban-American art and gifts. (p111)

Retro City Collectibles A fine selection of records, plus comic books, film posters and more. (p139)

Harold Golen Gallery Pop art with appeal for the anime/comic crowd. (p101)

Activities

Miami doesn't lack for ways to keep yourself busy. From sailing the teal waters to hiking through tropical undergrowth, yoga in the parks and (why not?) trapeze artistry above the city's head, the Magic City rewards those who want an active holiday.

Bicycling

The Miami-Dade County Parks and Recreation Department maintain a list of traffic-free cycling paths as well as downloadable maps on its website (www.miamidade.gov/parksmasterplan/bike-trails-map.asp). For less strenuous rides, try the side roads of South Beach or the shady streets of Coral Gables and Coconut Grove. Some good trails include the Old Cutler Trail, which starts at the traffic circle at Ingraham Terrace Park and continues south for 4 miles on to Pinecrest Gardens, passing Fairchild Tropical Garden and Matheson Hammock Park on the way. The Rickenbacker Causeway takes you up and over the bridge to Key Biscayne for an excellent workout combined with gorgeous water views (from the mainland to Bill Baggs State Park is about 7 miles). A bit further out, the Oleta River State Park has a challenging dirt trail with hills for off-road adventures. See p150 for bike rentals including Citi Bike (pictured) and trail-bike specialists Bike & Roll.

Running

Running is popular and the beach is very good for jogging, as it's flat, wide and hard-packed (apparently with amazingly good-looking runners). A great resource for races and special events is the Rub Club Network (www.runclubnetwork.com)

Some good places for a run include the Flamingo Park track, located east of Alton Rd between 11th St and 12th St,

LAZYLLAMA/SHUTTERSTOCK ©

for serious runners; Promenade in South Beach for its style; the boardwalk on Mid-Beach for great people-watching and scenery; and South Bayshore Dr in Coconut Grove for its shady banyan trees.

Diving & Snorkeling

Head to the Keys (about 70 miles south) or Biscayne National Park (40 miles south; www.nps.gov/bisc), in the southeastern corner of Dade county. If you don't have a car, dive operators in town lead organized day trips, taking you to colorful coral reefs like the John Pennekamp State Park in Key Largo.

Best Water Escapes

Virginia Key Beach North Point Park Look for manatees and bird life on a peaceful paddle off Virginia Key. (p113)

Venetian Pool A lovely spot to splash around. (p134)

Oleta River State Park A magical setting for kayaking or canoeing amid the mangroves. (p58)

Russian & Turkish Baths Old-school steam baths plunked straight out of the old country. (p57)

Best Hiking & Biking

Marjory Stoneman Douglas Biscayne Nature Center Take to the short nature trails for a look at South Florida's wild side. (p113)

Key Biscayne Hire a bike for the ride over the causeways and out along Key Biscayne. (p113)

Best Yoga

Barnacle Historic State Park Hosts 6:30pm yoga classes on Mondays and Wednesdays ($15) in a lovely outdoor setting. (p119)

Bayfront Park Free classes held outdoors at Tina Hills Pavilion, at the south end of the park. (p70)

Film, Theater & Dance

TRAVELVIEW/SHUTTERSTOCK©

Miami's arts scene draws from an enviable creative demographic base. Immigrants from around the world come here to create a better life, and in the process they've also created world-class art, live music and theater – all of it given a unique, sexy twist thanks to the sultry weather and sheer compressed diversity of South Florida.

Film & Theater

With such a diverse global audience here, you'll find plenty of intriguing foreign fare, as well as indie films and documentaries. Miami has a glut of art-house cinemas showing these sorts of films as well as plenty of Hollywood features. The city also has a small but vibrant theater scene. See www.southflorida theatre.com for a comprehensive direc-tory of playhouses in the region.

Best Performing Arts Venues

Adrienne Arsht Center for the Performing Arts World-class repertoire of Broadway shows, concerts, opera and ballet. (p68)

Olympia Theater Great venue for all types of shows and concerts. (pictured; p83)

New World Center Miami Beach's iconic concert hall. (p43)

Best Cinemas

Coral Gables Art Cinema Indie and foreign films in a 144-seat cinema. (p139)

Tower Theater In a gem of a deco building, managed by Miami-Dade College. (p108)

O Cinema Indie screenings in South Beach. (p51)

Best Theaters

Actors Playhouse A well-loved classic, in the heart of downtown Coral Gables. (p139)

Gablestage Thought-provoking works staged in the Biltmore. (p139)

Light Box at Goldman Warehouse Creative fare at a Wynwood incubator of the arts. (p100)

Music

Obviously, Miami's music scene is deeply influenced by Latin America and the Caribbean, but the sounds of those regions have blended with American hip-hop, Euro synthwave and a dozen other genres. Still, this is Miami; we're not kidding when we say we've heard reggaetón tracks pop off in the most inked up Miami punk clubs.

ALEXANDER TAMARGO/GETTY IMAGES©

Latin American Influences

Cuban salsa, Jamaican reggae, Dominican merengue and Spanish flamenco, plus mambo, rumba, cha-cha, calypso, Haitian konpa and every other music produced outside of the Anglophone Western Hemisphere finds a home, a studio and a dance team here. The best times to see ensemble Cuban bands is during celebrations such as Carnaval Miami, or at bars like Cafe La Trova.

Live Music

Miami's live music community has diversity and depth, but it can be overshadowed by the DJ/promotions scene of South Beach and parts of Downtown. The Miami New Times (www.miaminewtimes.com) is a good source of up-to-date listings. There's no one live-music neighborhood and there are no easy cliches; Spanish-language punk is as common as Anglophones trying to re-create *bossa nova*.

Best Live Music

Cafe La Trova This live Latin music venue has nailed the Old Havana dancehall vibe. (p109)

New World Center Miami Beach's premier spot for a classical music concert. (p43)

Ball & Chain Lovingly restored venue at the heart of Little Havana's cultural scene. (p109)

Wynwood Marketplace Merchant stalls and food kiosks arranged around a live performance stage. (p94)

Cubaocho A beautiful Little Havana spot for dancing, live music and general liveliness. (p111)

Museums

SONGQUAN DENG/SHUTTERSTOCK©

Miami has a treasure chest of great museums. Though the city is best known for its art, there are plenty of other outstanding realms to explore, from science and the biological world to urban design and the legacy of Miami's many immigrant communities.

Best Art Museums

Pérez Art Museum Miami A beautiful waterfront gallery that stages the top art exhibitions in Miami. (p66)

Wolfsonian-FIU An obligatory stop for anyone interested in 19th- and 20th-century design. (p42)

The Bass Outstanding collection of European masterpieces in a light-filled space. (p44)

Art Deco Museum Small South Beach gem that gives a great overview of Miami's architectural treasures. (p42)

Best Culture & History

HistoryMiami The best place in town to learn about the city's fascinating and complicated history. (p76)

Jewish Museum of Florida-FIU Learn about the deep Jewish ties to Miami's cultural life. (p44)

Coral Gables Museum A scrappy museum that celebrates the unique history of a master-planned Mediterranean-inspired village. (p136)

Best of the Rest

Patricia & Phillip Frost Museum of Science This celebrated new museum downtown has a sprawling collection of interactive exhibits. (p76)

Vizcaya Museum & Gardens Perusing the collection of 18th-century paintings and decorative items feels like stepping into old-world Europe. (pictured; p116)

World Erotic Art Museum A fascinating look at eroticism, from ancient sex manuals to Victorian peep-show photos. (p45)

Museum of Graffiti A deep dive into an original American school of urban art. (p94)

SEAN DRAKES/GETTY IMAGES©

Festivals & Events

Miami's warm weather and appetite for good times all pushes for a packed calendar of events. The only time the calendar really winds down is the hottest dog days of summer, which is also hurricane season, but even then monthly parties are still a popular way of blowing off steam.

Art Basel Miami Beach (www.artbasel.com/miami -beach; ☻early Dec) One of the most important international art shows in the world, this four-day fest features open-air art installations around town, special exhibitions at many galleries and outdoor film screenings.

Wynwood Life (☎305-461-2700; www.wynwoodlife. com; ☻Sep) A celebration of all things Wynwood, with live music and DJs, a big market of arts and crafts, fashion shows, food trucks, a culinary stage and a crew of talented street artists creating live installations.

Art Deco Weekend (☎305-672-2014; www. artdecoweekend.com; Ocean Dr, btwn 1st & 23rd Sts; ☻mid-Jan) This weekend fair features guided

tours, concerts, classic-auto shows, sidewalk cafes, arts and antiques.

Calle Ocho Festival (Carnaval Miami; www. carnavalmiami.com; ☻Mar) This massive street party (pictured) is the culmination of Carnaval Miami, a 10-day celebration of Latin culture.

Coconut Grove Arts Festival (www.coconut groveartsfest.com; Bayshore Dr, Coconut Grove; ☻late Feb) This three-day fair features works by more than 350 visual artists, plus concerts, dance and theater troupes, a culinary-arts component and a global village with world food.

Independence Day Celebration (Bayfront Park; ☻Jul 4) Excellent fireworks, a laser show and live music that draw more

than 100,000 people to breezy Bayfront Park.

Miami Beach Gay Pride (www.miamibeachgaypride. com; ☻Apr) Miami Beach proudly flies the rainbow flag high in this weekend festival that culminates in a colorful street parade along Ocean Dr.

Miami International Film Festival (☎305-237-3456; www.miami filmfestival.com; ☻Mar) A 10-day festival showcasing documentaries and features from all over the world at Miami cinemas.

Miami Museum Month (www.miamimuseummonth. com; ☻May) Held through the month of May, hang out in some of the best museums in the city for happy hours, special exhibitions and lectures.

Tours

BAILEYC1/SHUTTERSTOCK ©

Miami is a great city for exploring on your own, but for deeper insight, consider signing up for a guided tour. Highlights here include architecture strolls along South Beach, art-focused walks amid the galleries and painted urban landscape of Wynwood, and food tours where you get to taste your way around the globe.

Miami Design Preservation League (MDPL; 📞305-672-2014; www.mdpl.org; 1001 Ocean Dr; guided tours adult/student $30/25) Tells the stories and history behind the art-deco buildings in South Beach, with a lively guide.

Wynwood Art Walk (📞305-814-9290; www.wynwoodartwalk.com; tours from $29) Not to be confused with the monthly art celebration of the same name, this Wynwood Art Walk is actually a 90-minute guided tour taking you to some of the best gallery shows of the day, plus a look at some of the top street art around the 'hood.

Miami Food Tours (📞786-361-0991; www.miamifoodtours.com; 429 Lenox Ave; South Beach tour adult/child $58/35, Wynwood tour $75/55, Swooped with Forks $129/109; ⊙tours South Beach 11am & 4:30pm daily, Wynwood 10:30am Mon-Sat) Highly rated tour that explores various facets of the city – culture, history, art, and of course cuisine – while making stops at restaurants and cafes along the way.

Miami EcoAdventures (📞305-666-5885; www.miamidade.gov/ecoadventures; bike tours $5, kayaking & canoeing $30-45) Offers a variety of tours, including bike tours on Key Biscayne and canoe trips on the Oleta River, plus kayaking, snorkeling, walking and bird-watching.

History Miami Tours (📞305-375-1492; www.historymiami.org/city-tour; tours $30-60) Historian extraordinaire Dr Paul George leads fascinating walking tours, including culturally rich strolls through Little Haiti, Little Havana, Downtown and Coral Gables at twilight, plus the occasional boat trip to Stiltsville (pictured) and Key Biscayne.

Bike & Roll (📞305-604-0001; www.bikemiami.com; 210 10th St; rental per 2/4hr from $15/20, per day from $25, tours $49; ⊙9am-7pm) Miami is largely flat, the weather is warm, and the ocean is never far away. In other words, it's a great town for cycling. This outfit conducts several bike tours that show off themes from Wynwood graffiti to Miami Beach architecture.

For Free

It's no secret that Miami can quickly put a dent in the travel budget. Luckily, the city offers some excellent free attractions – from behind-the-scenes concert hall tours to some outstanding free art galleries. The star attraction is of course the beach, which is free and open to all.

MIA2YOU/SHUTTERSTOCK©

Art & Design

Wynwood Walls One of Miami's best-loved sights is an ever-changing installation of raw beauty. (p86)

De La Cruz Collection A stunning collection of works – always free to visit – in the Design District. (p91)

Bakehouse Art Complex Cutting-edge works by contemporary artists in Wynwood. (p94)

Pérez Art Museum Miami Take advantage of free admission days on the first Thursday and the second Saturday of the month. (p66)

Fly's Eye Dome A geodesic dome and iconic public sculpture tucked away in the Design District. (p91)

Locust Projects Often stages excellent art exhibitions. (p91)

Parks & Outdoor Attractions

SoundScape Park Catch free outdoor film screenings throughout the year in South Beach. (p43)

Wynwood Marketplace Stroll around the kiosks, listen to the live performances and soak up Wynwood. (p94)

South Pointe Park Head to the southernmost tip of Miami Beach for a family-friendly seaside relaxation spot. (pictured; p45)

Boardwalk The Miami Beach Boardwalk is an always entertaining mix of tourists, locals and sun seekers. (p58)

Bayfront Park Take a free yoga class on Mondays and Wednesdays at 6pm and Saturday at 9am. (p70)

Tours

Biltmore Hotel Explore the public spaces of this grand dame at your leisure. Or join a free tour on Sundays (1:30pm and 2:30pm). (p130)

Adrienne Arsht Center for the Performing Arts Offers free guided tours at noon on Mondays and Saturdays. (p68)

For Kids

FOTOLUMINATE LLC/SHUTTERSTOCK ©

Miami has loads of attractions for young travelers. You'll find lovely beaches, grassy parks, nature trails, megamalls, zoos and other animal-centric attractions. Plus, there's plenty of great snacks, from Italian-style gelato to Venezuelan arepas (corn cakes). There are also loads of family-friendly hotels and restaurants.

Beaches & Pools

Venetian Pool Spend the day splashing about in Miami's loveliest swimming pool. (p134)

South Pointe Park Ice-cream stands, soft grass, a beach and mini water park. (p45)

Boardwalk Fronts a family-friendly stretch of sand in Mid-Beach. (p58)

Crandon Park Pretty Key Biscayne spot with sand and nature trails. (pictured; p113)

Bill Baggs Cape Florida State Park Picnic tables front a pretty sweep of beach, plus scenic walks among the greenery. (p113)

Parks & Green Spaces

Bayfront Park Right in Downtown, with open spaces for running around, a good playground and outdoor dining nearby. (p70)

Oleta River State Park Huge park with waterfront access, plus canoe and kayak rental. (p58)

Marjory Stoneman Douglas Biscayne Nature Center Aquarium exhibits, short nature trails and monthly kid-focused outdoor activities. (p113)

Vizcaya Museum & Gardens Older children will appreciate the whimsy of this fairy-tale mansion and sprawling gardens. (p116)

Barnacle Historic State Park Outdoor paths and frequent family-friendly outdoor concerts. (p119)

Rainy Day Activities

Miami Children's Museum An indoor playland where kids can go on many imaginary adventures (including under the sea). (p77)

HistoryMiami Fascinating multimedia exhibits on Miami's history; there is even a display on pirates! (p76)

Patricia & Phillip Frost Museum of Science Aquarium, planetarium and hands-on exhibits exploring the wonders of the natural world. (p76)

LGBTIQ+

In Miami, the gay scene is so integrated it can be difficult to separate it from the straight one; popular hot spots include South Beach (where folks go to party), North Beach (where folks go to relax), and Wynwood and the Design District (where folks go for art galleries and activism...and to party, too).

MIA2YOU/SHUTTERSTOCK ©

Where to Go

The majority of dedicated, meat-market nightlife is in South Beach. The Upper East Side, which runs near Biscayne Bay east of Little Haiti, represents the edge of gentrification, and is a good area for casual LGBTIQ+-friendly hangout spaces. In the neighborhoods we cover, you'll find bars that cater to clientele of all diversities.

In early October Miami hosts the five-day Aqua Girl (www.aquagirl.org) festival – the largest charity event for the LBT community in the nation. Miami Beach Gay Pride (p21) is in April.

Best Travel Resources

LGBT Visitor Center (www.gogaymiami.com) The best single source for LGBTIQ+ Miami. Check the website for Pink Flamingo–certified hotels.

Miami Visitors Bureau (www.miamiandbeaches.com/things-to-do/travel-guides/gay-miami) A useful guide to gay life in the city.

Best Beaches

South Beach The area around 12th & Ocean Drive is popular with a mainly gay, male crowd. (p42)

Haulover Beach Park Parts of this beach are clothing optional, and all areas are LGBTIQ+ friendly. (p58)

Best LGBTIQ+ Bars & Brunches

Gramps In Wynwood, this amiable spot hosts plenty of drag shows and LGBTIQ+-friendly dance shows. (p100)

R House The drag brunch at this Wynwood bar is one of Miami's most beloved regular events. (p100)

Sweet Liberty Famous for its 'Birdcage Brunch', named for the iconic gay movie filmed here in South Beach. (p49)

Four Perfect Days

Day 1

ALEXANDREPHOTO7/SHUTTERSTOCK ©

Start with a morning stroll along **South Beach** (p42), then stop in the small **Art Deco Museum** (p42) for an overview of this iconic architectural district. Wander along Ocean Dr and see these deco beauties in person (or go on a guided tour with the **Miami Design Preservation League**; p46). For more deco insight, visit the **Wolfsonian-FIU** (p42).

Have lunch at the **11th St Diner** (pictured; p37), then take a stroll along Lincoln Rd, a pedestrian boulevard packed with architectural flourishes, shops, restaurants, models, people gawking at models, and so on.

For dinner, try **Chotto Matte** (p48) for Peruvian-Japanese cuisine and a very impressive dining room. Finish with drinks at **Sweet Liberty** (p49).

Day 2

TOMEI213/SHUTTERSTOCK ©

Start the day with espresso from **Panther Coffee** (p97) in Wynwood. Check out the murals at **Wynwood Walls** (p86), look for gifts at **Malaquita** (p101) and explore the **Margulies Collection at the Warehouse** (p94). Head to the **Museum of Graffiti** (p94) to contextualize the street art.

Spend the afternoon exploring **Pérez Art Museum Miami** (p66), which has some of the city's best contemporary art. Afterwards, head to **Bayfront Park** (p70), check out the Noguchi sculptures and join locals for a picnic.

Head back up to Wynwood for dinner at Asian food hall **1 800 Lucky** (p96), then catch some drinks at **Wood Tavern** (p99) or **Wynwood Marketplace** (pictured; p94).

Day 3

AGF/GETTY IMAGES ©

Spend the morning wandering the European gardens and art- and antique-filled interiors of **Vizcaya Museum & Gardens** (p116). Next, go over to Coconut Grove for shopping. **Barnacle Historic State Park** (p119) has attractive views.

Now head to Little Havana, stopping for lunch at **Doce Provisions** (p107) for contemporary Cuban cuisine. Check out the domino action in **Máximo Gómez Park** (pictured; p107). Stop for a fresh-squeezed pick-me-up juice at **Los Pinareños Frutería** (p108).

Have dinner at **El Nuevo Siglo** (p107), then catch some live music at **Cafe La Trova** (p109), where you can hear Latin jazz, flamenco, Cuban son and other styles.

Day 4

KARGRAR/SHUTTERSTOCK ©

Explore the **Fairchild Tropical Garden** (pictured; p128), with its rainforest, colorful butterflies and woodland paths. In Coral Gables, stroll along shop-lined Miracle Mile. Have a flat white and a lunch special at **Threefold** (p136).

If the weather is steamy, head to the **Venetian Pool** (p134) for an opulent dip. Otherwise, opt for the **Biltmore Hotel** (p130), a grand old beauty modeled on Seville's Giralda Tower.

Grab tapas at the Spanish contemporary restaurant **NIU Kitchen** (p77) in Downtown, then attend a show at the **Adrienne Arsht Center for the Performing Arts** (p68), capped off with some drinks at **Lost Boy** (p81) or **Baby Jane** (p82).

Need to Know

For detailed information, see Survival Guide (p147)

Currency
US dollars ($)

Language
English, Spanish

Visas
Required for most foreign visitors unless eligible for the Visa Waiver Program.

Money
ATMs are widely available, though most ATM withdrawals using out-of-state cards incur surcharges of $3 or so. Major credit cards are widely accepted.

Cell Phones
Local SIM cards can be used in European or Australian phones. Europe and Asia's GSM 900/1800 standard is incompatible with the USA's cell-phone systems. Check with your service provider about using your phone in the US.

Time
Eastern Time (GMT/UTC minus five hours)

Daily Budget

Budget: Less than $150
Hostel dorm: $30–50

Double in a budget hotel: $120

Meal from a food truck: $10–15

Citi Bike hire for an hour: $6.50

Happy hour drink special: from $5

Midrange: $150–300
Standard hotel room booked online: $150–250

Midrange dinner: around $30–50

Architectural walking tour: from $25

Craft cocktail in a lounge: $12–18

Top End: More than $300
Cover at bigger nightclubs: from $20

Dinner at an upscale restaurant: from $60

Day at a top spa: from $150

Kayak hire off Key Biscayne: $25 per hour

Advance Planning

One month before Book tickets at major venues (Miami Heat or Dolphins tickets, concerts at New World Center or Adrienne Arsht Center for the Performing Arts).

Two weeks before Reserve a table at any high-end restaurants you'd like to dine at.

One week before Check online for the latest restaurant and bar openings, as well as upcoming concerts and art exhibitions.

Arriving in Miami

✈ Miami International Airport

Taxis charge a flat rate for the 40-minute drive to South Beach ($35). The Miami Beach Airport Express (bus 150) costs $2.25 and makes stops all along Miami Beach, from 41st to the southern tip. SuperShuttle runs a shared-van service, costing about $22 to South Beach.

✈ Fort Lauderdale-Hollywood International Airport

GO Airport Shuttle runs shared vans to Miami, with prices around $25 to South Beach. A taxi costs about $75 (metered fare) to South Beach and $65 to Downtown.

Getting Around

🚗 Rental Car

Convenient, but parking can be expensive.

🚌 Bus

Extensive system, though slow for long journeys.

Ⓜ Metromover

Equal parts bus, monorail and train (pictured); helpful for getting around Downtown.

🚌 Trolley

Free service with various routes in Miami Beach, Downtown, Wynwood, Coconut Grove, Coral Gables, Little Havana and other neighborhoods (www.miamigov.com/trolley).

🚌 Train

Metrorail has one elevated line running from Hialeah through Downtown Miami and south to Kendall/Dadeland.

🚲 Citi Bike

Bike-sharing network in both Miami and Miami Beach. Easy to check out from a self-serve kiosk with a credit card.

Miami Neighborhoods

Coral Gables (p127)
Feels like a Mediterranean town dropped into greater Miami, with shopping on Miracle Mile, a Venetian pool and cultural theaters.

Little Havana (p103)
Stroll colorful Calle Ocho for a taste of Latin culture with its fine Cuban cooking, eye-catching storefronts and live music.

Cuban Memorial Boulevard Park ◉

Vizcaya Museum & Gardens ◉

Biltmore Hotel ◉

Coconut Grove (p115)
A peaceful waterfront neighborhood with tree-lined streets ripe for exploring and several gardens to visit for a nature fix.

Fairchild Tropical Garden ◉

Explore ◈
South Beach

South Beach (SoBe) is everything Miami is known for – the sparkling beach, beautiful art deco architecture, top-end boutiques and buzzing bars and restaurants. Still, there's more to this district than velvet ropes and high-priced lodging (though there's a lot of this too). You'll find some great down-to-earth bars, good eating and cool museums, all set against a backdrop of relentlessly attractive pastel deco architecture.

The Short List

○ **Art Deco Historic District (p36)** *Catching South Beach's art deco beauties at their most alluring.*

○ **South Beach (p42)** *People-watching on one of the world's most iconic beaches.*

○ **Wolfsonian-FIU (p42)** *Browsing gorgeous 19th- and 20th-century works on display at this highly respected museum dedicated to decorative arts and design.*

○ **Art Deco Museum (p42)** *Getting an overview of the area's architectural heritage.*

○ **New World Center (p43)** *Attending a performance inside a Frank Gehry concert hall.*

Getting There & Around

🚌 From Downtown, buses 119 and 120 go to South Beach via the MacArthur Causeway.

🚲 The Venetian Causeway has a separate lane for cyclists and the speed limit is low.

🚤 Water Taxi Miami provides ferry transport between South Beach and the Bayside Marketplace in Downtown Miami.

South Beach Map on p40

Lifeguard tower, South Beach ALEXANDER DEMYANENKO/SHUTTERSTOCK©

Top Sight 📷
Art Deco Historic District

The world-famous Art Deco Historic District of Miami Beach is pure exuberance: architecture of bold lines, whimsical tropical motifs and a color palette that evokes the beauty of Miami's landscape. Among the 800 deco buildings listed on the National Register of Historic Places, each design is different, and it's hard not to be captivated when strolling among these restored beauties from a bygone era.

◉ MAP P40, E4

Ocean Dr

Background

In the early 20th century, a few entrepreneurs began to transform a scrubby island into the resort city of Miami Beach, but in 1926 a hurricane left a devastating swath across much of South Florida. When it was time to rebuild, a bold new style of architecture had just burst onto the scene at a renowned fair known as the Exposition Internationale des Arts Décoratifs et Industriels Modernes held in Paris in 1925.

Over the next few years developers arrived in droves and Miami Beach became the epicenter of this ground-breaking new design (known then as 'art moderne' or 'modernistic'). Hundreds of new hotels were built during the 1930s to accommodate the influx of middle-class tourists flooding into Miami Beach.

Art Deco Style

The late 1920s and 1930s was an era of invention – of new automobiles, streamlined machines, radio antennae and cruise ships. Architects manifested these elements in strong vertical and horizontal lines, at times coupled with zigzags or sleek curves, all of which represented the bold forward march into the future.

In Miami Beach architects also incorporated more local motifs such as palm trees, flamingos and tropical plants. Nautical themes appeared too, with playful representations of ocean waves, sea horses, starfish and lighthouses. The style later became known as tropical deco.

Architects also came up with unique solutions to the challenges of building design in a hot, sun-drenched climate. Eyebrow-like ledges jutted over the windows, providing shade (and cooler inside temperatures), without obstructing the views.

The stretch of Ocean Dr between 11th and 14th Sts has a collection of striking art deco.

★ Top Tips

o Go early in the day when the crowds are thinnest and the light is best for taking pictures.

o For deeper insight into the architecture, take a guided walking tour offered daily by the Miami Design Preservation League (p46).

o Complete the deco experience by checking out the excellent exhibitions at the Art Deco Museum (p42) or the Wolfsonian-FIU (p42), both nearby.

✕ Take a Break

Stop in for sandwiches and a cold drink at La Sandwicherie (p48).

Complete the journey into the past with a meal in the **11th Street Diner** (☎305-534-6373; www.eleventhstreet diner.com; 1065 Washington Ave; mains $10-20; ⏰7am-midnight Mon & Tue, 24hr Wed-Sun), set in a 1940s train car.

Walking Tour 🥾

Art Deco Architecture

The art deco architecture that defines South Beach helped to establish the areas as a go-to tourism destination in the early 20th century, and was crucial to efforts to revitalize the era in the 1980s. The art deco hotels that line Ocean Drive and Collins Ave are a pastel testament to the cultural (and commercial!) benefits of prioritizing preservation.

Walk Facts

Start Art Deco Museum
End Hotel of South Beach
Length 1.2 miles; two to three hours

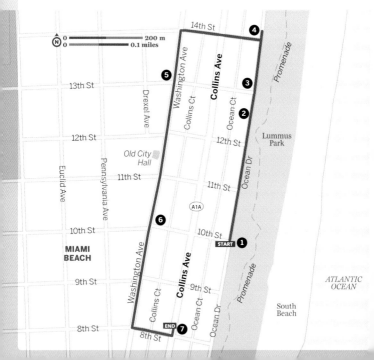

❶ Art Deco Museum

Start at the **Art Deco Museum** (p42), at the corner of Ocean Dr and 10th St (named Barbara Capitman Way here after the founder of the Miami Design Preservation League). Step in for an exhibit on art deco style, then head out and go north along Ocean Dr.

❷ The Leslie

Stay on the beach side of Ocean Dr as you walk north for the best views of the buildings. As you stroll, you'll see many fine examples of deco hotels, including the eye-catching **Leslie**, a boxy shape with eyebrows (cantilevered sun shades) wrapped around the side of the building.

❸ The Cardozo

Cross 13th St and have a look at the **Cardozo** (1300 Ocean Dr), one of the first deco hotels saved by the Miami Design Preservation League. Its beautiful lines and curves evoke a classic automobile from the 1930s. Back in the day, this property was owned by one Ms Gloria Estefan.

❹ Winter Haven Hotel

Up at 14th St, peek inside the sun-drenched **Winter Haven Hotel** (www.winterhavenhotelsobe.com; 1400 Ocean Dr) to see its fabulous floors of terrazzo, made of stone chips set in mortar then polished when dry. Be sure to look up and check out the deco ceiling lamps, with their sharp, retro sci-fi lines. The Winter Haven dates back to 1939 and was designed by Albert Anis, an icon of deco style.

❺ Post Office

Turn down 14th St east to Washington Ave and the US **Post Office** (1300 Washington Ave; ⏰8am-5pm Mon-Fri, 8:30am-2pm Sat) at 13th St. It was built in Depression Modern style, with a domed cupola and decorative ceiling in the lobby. Note the wall mural depicting a scene of Spanish explorer Hernando de Soto encountering/battling Native Americans.

❻ Wolfsonian-FIU

Walk east to the imposing **Wolfsonian-FIU** (p42), an excellent museum of design, formerly the Washington Storage Company. Wealthy snowbirds of the '30s stashed their pricey belongings here before returning north. Today the museum provides invaluable contextual insight into local aesthetics and design history.

❼ Hotel of South Beach

Keep walking along Washington Ave, turn left on 8th St and then continue north along Collins Ave to the **Hotel of South Beach** (www.thehotelofsouthbeach.com; 801 Collins Ave), featuring an interior and roof deck by Todd Oldham.

South Beach

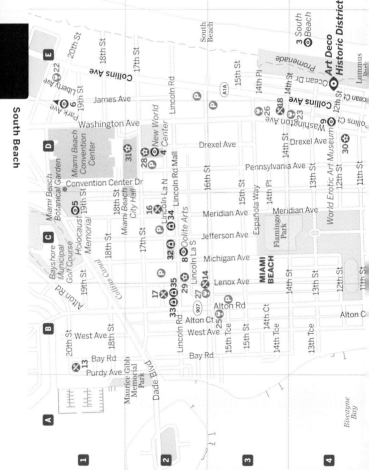

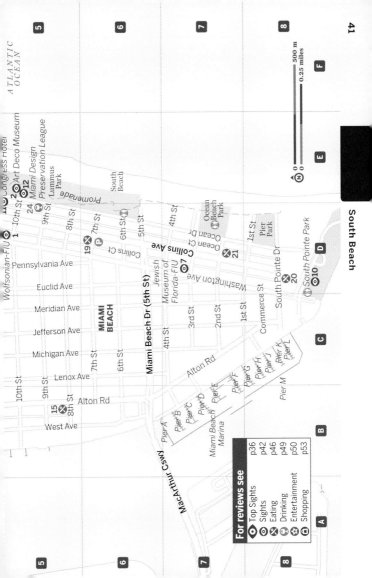

South Beach

ATLANTIC
OCEAN

Congress Hotel
1
Art Deco Museum
2
Miami Design
Preservation League
24
12
Lummus
Park
South
Beach
Promenade

Wolfsonian-FIU
1
10th St
9th St
8th St
7th St
6th St
5th St
4th St

Jewish
Museum of
Florida-FIU
7

Ocean
Beach
Park

Pennsylvania Ave
Euclid Ave
Meridian Ave
Jefferson Ave
Michigan Ave
Lenox Ave

19
Collins Ct
Collins Ave

Ocean Ct
Ocean Dr
21

Washington Ave

1st St
Pier
Park

South Pointe Park
South Pointe Dr
20
10

MIAMI
BEACH

Miami Beach Dr (5th St)

4th St
3rd St
2nd St
1st St
Commerce St

7th St
6th St

Alton Rd

10th St
9th St
8th St
Alton Rd
15

MacArthur Cswy

West Ave

Pier A
Pier B
Pier C
Pier D
Pier E
Pier F
Pier G
Pier H
Pier J
Pier K
Pier L
Pier M

Miami Beach
Marina

500 m
0.25 miles

For reviews see	
Top Sights	p36
Sights	p42
Eating	p46
Drinking	p49
Entertainment	p50
Shopping	p53

Sights

Wolfsonian-FIU   MUSEUM

1 ◉ MAP P40, D5

Visit this excellent design museum early in your stay to put the aesthetics of Miami Beach into context. It's one thing to see how wealth, leisure and the pursuit of beauty manifest, but it's another to understand the roots and shadings of local artistic movements. By chronicling the interior evolution of everyday life, the Wolfsonian reveals how these trends manifested architecturally in SoBe's exterior deco.

Take a look at the Wolfsonian's own noteworthy architectural features with its Gothic-futurist angles and lion-head-studded grand elevator. (☎305-531-1001; www.wolfsonian.org; 1001 Washington Ave; adult/child $12/8, 6-9pm Fri free; ⏰10am-6pm Mon, Tue, Thu & Sat, to 9pm Fri, noon-6pm Sun)

Art Deco Museum   MUSEUM

2 ◉ MAP P40, E5

This small museum is one of the best places in town for an enlightening overview of the art deco district. Through videos, photography, models and other displays, you'll learn about the pioneering work of Barbara Baer Capitman, who helped save these buildings from certain destruction back in the 1970s, and her collaboration with Leonard Horowitz, the talented artist who designed the

pastel color palette that became an integral part of the design visible today.

The museum also touches on other key architectural styles in Miami, including Mediterranean Revival (typefied by the Villa Casa Casuarina at 1116 Ocean Dr) and the post-deco boom of MiMo (Miami Modern), which emerged after WWII, and is particularly prevalent in North Miami Beach. The guided art deco tour is $30 per person and takes around two hours (10:30am daily, plus 6:30pm Thursday) touching on art deco, MiMo and Mediterranean Revival movements. (☎305-672-2014; www.mdpl.org; 1001 Ocean Dr; admission free; ⏰10am-5pm Tue-Sun)

South Beach   BEACH

3 ◉ MAP P40, E4

When most people think of Miami Beach, they envision South Beach (SoBe), a label that applies to both the beach itself and the neighborhood that adjoins it. The latter includes clubs, bars, restaurants and a distinctive veneer of art-deco architecture. The beach is a sweep of golden sands, dotted with colorful deco-style lifeguard stations and countless souls uploading panorama shots to their social media platforms. The shore gets crowded in high season (December to March) and most weekends.

You can escape the masses by avoiding the densest parts of the beach (5th to 15th Sts) – heading south of 5th street, to the area known as SoFi, is a good means of eluding the crowds. Keep in mind that there's no alcohol (or pets) allowed on the sand. (Ocean Dr; ⏱5am-midnight)

New World Center

NOTABLE BUILDING

4 ◉ MAP P40, D2

Designed by Frank Gehry, this performance hall rises majestically out of a manicured lawn just above Lincoln Rd. Not unlike the ethereal power of the music within, the glass-and-steel facade encases characteristically Gehry-esque sail-like shapes that help create the magnificent acoustics and add to the futuristic quality of the concert hall. The grounds form a 2.5-acre public park aptly known as **SoundScape Park** (www.nws. edu; 500 17th St).

Some performances inside the center are projected outside via a 7000-sq-ft projection wall (the so-called WALLCAST), which might make you feel like you're in the classiest open-air theater on the planet. Reserve ahead for a 45-minute guided tour. (⏴305-680-5866, tours 305-428-6776; www. nws.edu/new-world-center; 500 17th St; tours $5; ⏱tours 4pm Tue & Thu, 1pm Fri, 3pm Sat)

Holocaust Memorial

MEMORIAL

5 ◉ MAP P40, C1

Even for a Holocaust piece, this memorial is particularly powerful. With more than 100 sculptures,

New World Center, designed by architect Frank Gehry

its centerpiece is the *Sculpture of Love and Anguish,* an enormous, oxidized bronze arm that bears an Auschwitz tattoo number – chosen because it was never issued at the camp. Terrified camp prisoners scale the sides of the arm, trying to pass their loved ones, including children, to safety only to see them later massacred, while below lie figures of all ages in various poses of suffering. (www.holocaustmmb.org; cnr Meridian Ave & Dade Blvd; ☽9:30am-10pm)

The Bass   MUSEUM

6 ◎ MAP P40, D1

The best art museum in Miami Beach has a playfully futuristic facade, a crisp interplay of lines and a bright, white-walled space – like an Orthodox church on a space-age Greek isle. All designed, by the way, in 1930 by Russell Pancoast (grandson of John A Collins, who lent his name to Collins Ave).

Biking South Beach

One of the best ways to get around South Beach is by bicycle. The bike-sharing network Citi Bike has dozens of kiosks around, and checking out a bike is as easy as swiping a credit card, grabbing a bike and pedaling off. There's also a handy iPhone app (Citi Bike Miami) that shows nearby bike stations.

The collection isn't shabby either: there is a focus on cutting-edge contemporary art, although some temporary exhibitions showcase older work.

The museum forms one point of the Collins Park Cultural Center triangle, which also includes the three-story **Miami City Ballet** (☏305-929-7010; www.miamicity ballet.org; 2200 Liberty Ave) and the lovingly inviting Miami Beach Regional Library, which is a great place for free wifi. (☏305-673-7530; www.thebass.org; 2100 Collins Ave; adult/child $15/8; ☽10am-5pm Wed-Sun)

Jewish Museum of Florida-FIU   MUSEUM

7 ◎ MAP P40, D7

Housed in a 1936 Orthodox synagogue that served Miami's first congregation, this small museum chronicles the large contribution Jews have made to the state of Florida. After all, it could be said that while Cubans made Miami, Jews made Miami Beach, both physically and culturally. Yet there were times when Jews were barred from the American Riviera they carved out of the sand, and this museum tells that story, along with some amusing anecdotes (like seashell Purim dresses).

There are also walking tours of the area that take in famous local Jewish landmarks and businesses, as well as foodie tours of local Jewish restaurants

Secret Garden

The lush but little-known **Miami Beach Botanical Garden** (Map p40, D1; ☎305-673-7256; www.mbgarden.org; 2000 Convention Center Dr; free, suggested donation $2; ☺9am-5pm Tue-Sun) consists of 2.6 acres of plantings. It is operated by the Miami Beach Garden Conservancy and is a veritable green haven in the midst of the urban jungle – an oasis of palm trees, flowering hibiscus trees and glassy ponds. It's a great spot for a picnic. While touring the garden, you can dial ☎305-423-1525 for a free self-guided tour.

(three-hour tour including food $48; two-hour tour without food $20). (☎305-672-5044; www.jmof.fiu.edu; 301 Washington Ave; adult/student & senior $12/8, Sat free; ☺10am-5pm Tue-Sun, closed Mon & Jewish holidays)

Oolite Arts
GALLERY

8 MAP P40, C2

Once known as ArtCenter/South Florida South Beach, this exhibition space includes some 52 artists' studios, many of which are open to the public. Oolite also offers an exciting lineup of classes and lectures. The facility is scheduled to move to 75 NW 72nd St (in Little Haiti) in 2022.

The residences are reserved for artists who do not have major exposure, so this is a good place to spot up-and-coming talent. Monthly rotating exhibitions keep the presentation fresh and pretty avant-garde. (☎305-674-8278; https://oolitearts.org; 924 Lincoln Rd, 2nd fl; ☺noon-6pm Mon-Fri, 1-6pm Sat & Sun)

World Erotic Art Museum
MUSEUM

9 ◎ MAP P40, D4

The World Erotic Art Museum has a frankly staggering collection of erotica, including sexually charged pieces by Rembrandt and Picasso, ancient sex manuals, Victorian peep-show photos, the oversized sculpted genitals used as a murder weapon in *A Clockwork Orange*, and an elaborate four-poster (four-phallus rather) Kama Sutra bed, with carvings depicting various ways (138 in fact) to get intimate. The museum dates back to 2005, when Naomi Wilzig turned her 5000-piece collection into a South Beach mainstay. (☎305-532-9336; www.weam.com; 1205 Washington Ave; over 18yr $15; ☺11am-10pm Mon-Thu, to midnight Fri-Sun)

South Pointe Park
PARK

10 ◎ MAP P40, D8

The very southern tip of Miami Beach has been converted into a

Surfing
South Beach

SoBe Surf (📞 321-926-6571; www.sobesurf.com; group/private lessons from $70/120) offers surf lessons both in Miami Beach and in Cocoa Beach, where there tends to be better waves. Instruction on Miami Beach usually happens around South Point. All bookings are done by phone or email.

lovely park, replete with manicured grass for lounging and warm, scrubbed-stone walkways, as well as a tiny water park for the kids. There's also a restaurant and refreshment stand for all the folks who want to enjoy the great weather and teal ocean views minus the South Beach strutting. (📞 305-673-7779; 1 Washington Ave; ⏰ sunrise-10pm; 👫 🐾)

Congress Hotel   ARCHITECTURE

11 ◎ MAP P40, E5

Close to 11th St, the Congress Hotel is an art-deco classic, displaying perfect symmetry in its three-story facade. It has window-shading eyebrows and a long marquee down the middle that's reminiscent of the grand movie palaces of the 1930s. (1052 Ocean Dr)

Miami Design
Preservation League   WALKING

12 ◎ MAP P40, E5

The Miami Design Preservation League tells the stories and history behind the art-deco buildings in South Beach. The lively regular guided tours last 90 minutes. It

also offers tours of Jewish Miami Beach, Gay & Lesbian Miami Beach and tours of Mediterranean architecture and the MiMo district by request. Check the website for details and for tour days and times. (MDPL; 📞 305-672-2014; www.mdpl.org; 1001 Ocean Dr; guided tours adult/student $30/25)

Eating

Pubbelly   FUSION $$

13 ✖ MAP P40, B1

A mix of Asian and Latin flavors, Pubbelly serves hip fusion takes on small plates, and sushi such as grilled miso black cod with spring onions, beef tartare rolls with mustard and truffle poached egg, and Japanese fried chicken with kimchi. Super-popular and decently priced, it's a South Beach foodie spot that delivers. (📞 305-532-7555; http://pubbellyglobal.com; 1424 20th St; plates $9-24; ⏰ noon-11pm Sun-Thu, to midnight Fri & Sat; ✎)

Yardbird   SOUTHERN US $$

14 ✖ MAP P40, B2

Yardbird has earned a die-hard following for its haute Southern comfort food. The kitchen churns out some nice shrimp and grits, St Louis-style pork ribs, charred okra, and biscuits with smoked brisket, but it's most famous for its supremely good plate of fried chicken, spiced watermelon and waffles with bourbon maple syrup.

The setting is a shabby-chic interior of distressed wood, painted white brick columns, wicker basket-type lamps and big windows for taking in the passing street scene. (☏305-538-5220; www.runchickenrun.com; 1600 Lenox Ave; mains $18-38; ☺11am-midnight Mon-Fri, from 9am Sat & Sun; ☝)

Macchialina
ITALIAN $$

15 ✖ MAP P40, B5

This buzzing Italian trattoria has all the right ingredients for a terrific night out; namely great service and beautifully turned-out cooking, served in a warm rustic-chic interior of exposed brick and chunky wood tables. (☏305-534-2124; www.macchialina.com; 820 Alton Rd; mains $21-40)

Lincoln Eatery
FOOD HALL $

16 ✖ MAP P40, C2

It's easy to feel overwhelmed with choice in South Beach, which is why we love the Lincoln Eatery. OK, to be fair, this is a food hall, so there are still a lot of choices: taco spots, sushi counters, even a kosher barbecue stand. But at least all of these are concentrated in one easy-to-navigate arcade. (☏305-695-8700; www.thelincolneatery.com; 723 Lincoln Ln N; mains $8-17; ☺8am-10pm Mon-Thu, to 11pm Fri-Sun)

Fried chicken, spiced watermelon and waffles at Yardbird

ELIZABETH BEARD/GETTY IMAGES©

Chotto Matte

PERUVIAN $$$

17 MAP P40, B2

Chotto Matte is a strong contender for most physically beautiful restaurant in Miami, and that's saying something in this city of impressive design. Peruvian-Japanese cuisine – such as avocado doused with a truffle ponzu or beef in a spicy teriyaki sauce – is served in a roofless space that encloses a tropical garden. Even if you're not hungry, pop by for a drink to gawk at the layout. (☑ 305-690-0743; https://chotto-matte.com; 1664 Lenox Ave; small plates $13-29, mains $18-55; ☺ 4pm-midnight Mon-Fri, noon-1am Sat & Sun; ☝)

La Sandwicherie

SANDWICHES $

18 MAP P40, D3

Closed for just a few hours each day, this boxcar-long eatery does a roaring trade in filling baguette sandwiches sold at rock-bottom prices. Ingredients are fairly classic: roast beef, smoked salmon, avocado or combos like prosciutto with mozzarella, though you can load up with toppings for a deliciously satisfying meal.

Seating is limited to stools lining the restaurant's outside counter, but you can always get it to go and head to the beach. (☑ 305-532-8934; www.lasandwicherie.com; 229 14th St; mains $6-11; ☺ 7am-5am; ☝)

Puerto Sagua

CUBAN $

19 MAP P40, D6

Puerto Sagua challenges the US diner with this reminder: Cubans can greasy-spoon with the best of them. If you're never leaving South Beach, at least get a taste of authentic Cuban cuisine at this beloved institution, which has been slinging hash since 1962. Portions of favorites such as *picadillo* (spiced ground beef) are enormous. (☑ 305-673-1115; 700 Collins Ave; mains $8-18; ☺ 7:30am-2am)

Lilikoi

CAFE $$

20 MAP P40, D8

Head to the quieter, southern end of South Beach for healthy, mostly organic and veg-friendly dishes at this laid-back, indoor-outdoor spot. Start the morning off with big bowls of açai and granola or bagels with lox (and eggs Benedict on weekends); or linger over kale Caesar salads, mushroom risotto and falafel wraps at lunch. (☑ 305-763-8692; www.lilikoiorganicliving.com; 500 S Pointe Dr; mains $12-21; ☺ 8am-7pm Mon-Wed, to 8:30pm Thu-Sun; ☝)

Escaping the Crowds 🍽

Ocean Dr can feel a bit cheesy. Expect high prices and a circus-like feel to the dining or drinking experience if you take a seat here. To escape the mayhem, head to spots like Sunset Harbour or SoFi (south of Fifth), where you'll find a more local crowd and generally much higher quality when it comes to food and drink.

Big Pink
DINER $$

21 🍴 MAP P40, D7

Big Pink does American comfort food with joie de vivre and a dash of whimsy. The Americana menu is consistently good throughout the day; pulled Carolina pork holds the table next to a nicely done Reuben. The interior is somewhere between a '50s sock hop and a South Beach club; expect to be seated at a long communal table. (📞 305-532-4700; https://myles restaurantgroup.com/big-pink; 157 Collins Ave; mains $13-26; ⏰ 8am-midnight Mon-Wed, to 2am Thu, to 5am Fri & Sat)

Drinking

Sweet Liberty
BAR

22 🍸 MAP P40, E1

A much-loved local haunt near Collins Park, Sweet Liberty has all the right ingredients for a fun night out: friendly, easygoing bartenders who whip up excellent cocktails (try a mint julep), great happy-hour specials (including 75¢ oysters) and a relaxed crowd. The space is huge, with flickering candles, a long wooden bar and the odd band adding to the cheer.

There's also decent food ($6 to $31) on hand, from crab toast and cauliflower nachos to brisket sandwiches and beet and farro risotto. (📞 305-763-8217; www.mysweet liberty.com; 237 20th St; ⏰ 4pm-5am Mon-Sat, from noon Sun)

Mac's Club Deuce Bar
BAR

23 🍸 MAP P40, D4

The oldest bar in Miami Beach (established in 1926), the Deuce is a real neighborhood bar and hype-free zone. It's just straight-up seediness, which depending on your outlook can be quite refreshing. Plan to see everyone from tourists to drag queens to off-shift bar staff – some hooking up, some talking rough, all having a good time. (📞 305-531-6200; www.macsclubdeuce.com; 222 14th St; ⏰ 8am-5am)

Mango's Tropical Café
BAR

24 🍸 MAP P40, D5

Visitors from across the globe mix things up at this famous bar on Ocean Dr. Every night feels like a celebration, with a riotously fun vibe, and plenty of entertainment: namely minimally dressed staff dancing on the bar, doing Michael Jackson impersonations, shimmy-ing in feather headdresses or show-ing off some amazing salsa moves. It's a kitschy good time, which doesn't even take into consid-eration the small dance floor and stage in the back, where brassy Latin bands get everyone moving. (📞 305-673-4422; www.mangos.com; 900 Ocean Dr; $10, dinner & show ticket $26; ⏰ 11:45am-5am)

Bodega
COCKTAIL BAR

25 🍸 MAP P40, B3

Bodega looks like your average cool-kid Mexican joint – serving

Outdoor Screenings

From October through May, **SoundsScape Park** has weekly film screenings (currently Wednesdays at 8pm) – usually cult classics. Located outside of the New World Center, a 7000-sq-ft projection plays on the Frank Gehry–designed concert hall. In addition, some performances happening inside the hall are projected simultaneously outside. Bring a picnic and enjoy the show.

delicious tacos ($3 to $5) from a converted Airstream trailer to a party-minded crowd. But there's actually a bar hidden behind that blue porta-potty door on the right. Head inside (or join the long line on weekends) to take in a bit of old-school glam in a sprawling drinking den. (📞305-704-2145; www.bodegataqueria.com; 1220 16th St; ⏰noon-5am)

Kill Your Idol   BAR

26 MAP P40, D3

Kill Your Idol is a lovable hipster dive, with graffiti and shelves full of retro bric-a-brac covering the walls, plus drag shows on Monday and DJs spinning danceable old-school grooves. The crowd is a mix of cool-kid locals and fashionable out-of-towners. (📞305-672-1852; www.facebook.com/killyouridolmiami; 222 Española Way; ⏰8pm-5am)

Abbey Brewery   MICROBREWERY

27 MAP P40, B2

The oldest brewpub in South Beach is on the untouristed end of South Beach (near Alton Rd). It's friendly and packed with folks listening to throwback hits (grunge, '80s new wave) and slinging back some excellent homebrew: give Father Theo's stout or the Immaculate IPA a try. (📞305-538-8110; www.abbeybrewinginc.com; 1115 16th St; ⏰1pm-5am)

Entertainment

New World Symphony   CLASSICAL MUSIC

28 MAP P40, D2

Housed in the New World Center (p43) – a funky explosion of cubist lines and geometric curves, fresh white against the blue Miami sky – the acclaimed New World Symphony (NWS) holds performances from October to May. The deservedly heralded NWS serves as a three- to four-year preparatory program for talented musicians from prestigious music schools. (📞305-680-5866; www.nws.edu; 500 17th St)

Colony Theatre   PERFORMING ARTS

29 MAP P40, C2

The Colony was built in 1935 and was the main cinema in upper South Beach before it fell into disrepair in the mid-20th century. It was renovated and revived in 1976 and now boasts 465 seats and great acoustics. It's an absolute art-deco gem, with a classic marquee and Inca-style crenelations, and now serves as a major venue for performing arts. (📞305-674-1040, box office 800-211-1414; www.colonymb.org; 1040 Lincoln Rd)

O Cinema South Beach

CINEMA

30 MAP P40, D4

This much-loved nonprofit cinema screens indie films, foreign films and documentaries. You'll find thought-provoking works you won't see elsewhere. The venue itself is a hybrid theater/bookstore/library that occupies the old Miami Beach city hall, built in 1927 by real-estate mogul Carl Fischer. (📞786-471-3269; www.o-cinema.org/venue/o-cinema-south-beach; 1130 Washington Ave)

Fillmore Miami Beach

PERFORMING ARTS

31 MAP P40, D2

Built in 1951, South Beach's premier showcase for touring Broadway shows, orchestras and other big musical productions has 2700 seats and excellent acoustics. Jackie Gleason chose to make the theater his home for the long-running 1960s TV show, but now you'll find an eclectic lineup: Catalan pop or indie rock one night, the comedian Bill Maher or an over-the-top vaudeville group the next. (📞305-673-7300; www.fillmoremb.com; 1700 Washington Ave)

Colony Theatre

Rise of a
Beachside City

It's always been the weather that's attracted Miami's two most prominent species: developers and tourists. But it wasn't the sun per se that got people moving here – it was an ice storm. The great Florida freeze of 1895 wiped out the state's citrus industry; at the same time, widowed Julia Tuttle bought out parcels of land that would become modern Miami, and Henry Flagler was building his Florida East Coast Railroad. Tuttle offered to split her land with Flagler if he extended the railway to Miami, but the train man didn't pay her any heed until north Florida froze over and Tuttle sent him an 'I told you so' message: an orange blossom clipped from her Miami garden.

The rest is a history of boom, bust, dreamers and opportunists. Generally, Miami has grown in leaps and bounds following major world events and natural disasters. Hurricanes (particularly the deadly Great Miami Hurricane of 1926) have wiped away the town, but it just keeps bouncing and building back better than before. In the late 19th and early 20th centuries, Miami earned a reputation for attracting design and city-planning mavericks such as George Merrick, who fashioned the artful Mediterranean village of Coral Gables, and James Deering, designer of the fairy-tale Vizcaya mansion.

20th-Century Growth

Miami Beach blossomed in the early 20th century when Jewish developers recognized the potential American Riviera in their midst. Those hoteliers started building resorts that were branded with a distinctive art-deco facade by daring architects willing to buck the more staid aesthetics of the northeast. The world wars brought soldiers who were stationed at nearby naval facilities, many of whom liked the sun and decided to stay. Latin American and Caribbean revolutions introduced immigrants from the other direction, most famously from Cuba. Cuban immigrants arrived in two waves: first, the anti-Castro types of the '60s, and those looking for a better life since the late 1970s, such as the arrivals on the 1980 Mariel Boatlift during a Cuban economic crisis. The glam and overconsumption of the 1980s, as shown in movies like *Scarface* and *Miami Beach*, attracted a certain breed of the rich and beautiful, and their associated models, designers, hoteliers and socialites, all of whom transformed South Beach into the beautiful beast it is today.

Shopping

Books & Books BOOKS

32 🔒 MAP P40, C2

Stop in this fantastic indie bookstore for an excellent selection of new fiction, beautiful art and photography books, award-winning children's titles and more. The layout – a series of elegantly furnished rooms – invites endless browsing, and there's a good restaurant and cafe out the front of the store. (📞305-532-3222; www.booksandbooks.com; 927 Lincoln Rd; ⏱11am-9pm)

Taschen BOOKS

33 🔒 MAP P40, B2

An incredibly well-stocked collection of art, photography, design and coffee-table books from this high-quality illustrated-books publisher. Check out David Hockney's color-rich art books, the *New Erotic Photography* (always a great conversation starter) and Annie Liebovitz's witty society portraits. (📞305-538-6185; www.taschen.com; 1117 Lincoln Rd; ⏱11am-9pm Mon-Thu, to 10pm Fri & Sat, noon-9pm Sun)

Havaianas FASHION & ACCESSORIES

34 🔒 MAP P40, C2

The well-known Brazilian flip-flop (thong) brand serves up lots of different colors and styles (with plenty of recognizable Disney characters for the kids) at their popular shop on Lincoln Rd. You can also add custom embellishments – tiny hearts, diamonds, rhinestones and fleur de lys – to the straps. (📞786-477-6161; https://us.havaianas.com; 831 Lincoln Rd; ⏱10am-10pm Mon-Thu, to 11pm Fri & Sat, 11am-9pm Sun)

Alchemist FASHION & ACCESSORIES

35 🔒 MAP P40, B2

Inside one of Lincoln Rd's most striking buildings, this high-end boutique has a wild collection of artful objects, including Warhol-style soup-can candles, heavy gilded corkscrews, Beats headphones by Dr Dre, and mirrored circular sunglasses that are essential for the beach. The clothing here tends to be fairly avant-garde (straight from the runway it seems). Try out your garments in front of huge video screens of crashing waves and other tropical scenes. (📞305-531-4815; 1111 Lincoln Rd; ⏱11am-8pm)

Explore ◈
North Beach

If you're after fewer people along a gorgeous strip of sand that more than matches South Beach, then North Beach is for you. Instead of art deco, you'll find the so-called MiMo (Miami Modern) style of grand buildings constructed in the post-WWII boom days. There's good-quality eating and drinking, peppered amid immigrant communities from across Latin America and Europe.

The Short List

○ **Boardwalk (p58)** *Taking a mid-morning stroll along Mid-Beach's lush walkway, followed by a loll on the beach.*

○ **Oleta River State Park (p58)** *Looking for soaring eagles and other wildlife while kayaking inside the largest reserve in Miami.*

○ **Haulover Beach Park (p58)** *Playing in the waves off one of North Miami's prettiest beaches.*

○ **Russian & Turkish Baths (p57)** *Heading to the banya for a bit of old-school relaxation.*

○ **Faena Forum (p57)** *Admiring this wonderfully designed cultural center, ideally at an event or show.*

Getting There & Around

🚌 Some buses, including routes 119 and 120, zip along (traffic permitting) Collins Ave connecting South Beach and points north.

🚲 There are many Citi Bike stations here, but you'll have to take busy Collins Ave or Indian Creek Dr to reach northern points.

🚗 Finding parking is a little less tricky than down in South Beach.

North Beach Map on p56

Haulover Beach Park (p58) MIA2YOU/SHUTTERSTOCK©

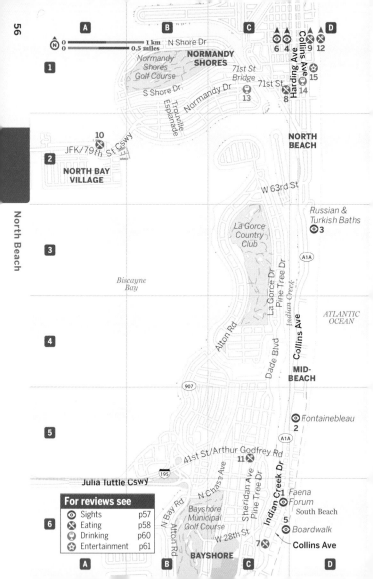

NORMANDY SHORES

Normandy Shores Golf Course

N Shore Dr

S Shore Dr

Normandy Dr

Trouville Esplanade

71st St Bridge

71st St

⊗ 8

⊙ 6 ⊙ 4

Collins Ave

⊗ 9 ⊗ 12

Harding Ave

☆ 15

⊗ 14

🚉 13

JFK/79th St Cswy

⊗ 10

NORTH BAY VILLAGE

NORTH BEACH

W 63rd St

Biscayne Bay

La Gorce Country Club

Russian & Turkish Baths ⊙ 3

La Gorce Dr

Pine Tree Dr

Indian Creek

A1A

Collins Ave

Alton Rd

ATLANTIC OCEAN

Dade Blvd

MID-BEACH

(907)

Fontainebleau ⊙ 2

A1A

Julia Tuttle Cswy

195

41st St/Arthur Godfrey Rd

⊗ 11

N Chase Ave

Sheridan Ave

Pine Tree Dr

Indian Creek Dr

Faena Forum ⊙ 1

South Beach

Boardwalk ⊙ 5

Collins Ave

⊗ 7

N Bay Rd

Alton Rd

Bayshore Municipal Golf Course

W 28th St

BAYSHORE

🔼 N 0 ⸻ 1 km
     0 ⸻ 0.5 miles

Sights

Faena Forum
CULTURAL CENTER

1 MAP P56, C6

This cultural center has been turning heads since its opening in late 2016. The circular Rem Koolhaas–designed building features rooms for performances, exhibitions, lectures and other events. Check the website to see what's coming up. (305-534-8800; www.faena.com; Collins Ave & 33rd St)

Fontainebleau
HISTORIC BUILDING

2 MAP P56, D5

As you proceed north on Collins, the condos and apartment buildings grow in grandeur and embellishment until you enter an area nicknamed Millionaire's Row. The most fantastic jewel in this glittering crown is the Fontainebleau hotel. The hotel – mainly the pool, which has since been renovated – features in Brian de Palma's classic *Scarface*.

This iconic 1954 leviathan is a brainchild of the great Miami Beach architect Morris Lapidus

and has undergone many renovations; in some ways, it is utterly different from its original form, but it retains that early glamour. (www.fontainebleau.com; 4441 Collins Ave)

Russian & Turkish Baths
MASSAGE

3 MAP P56, D3

This is an excellent spot for getting reasonably priced wellness treatments in a local – very local – environment. Go for a *platza*: a treatment where you're beaten by oak-leaf brooms called *venik* in a lava-hot spa (for $40). The Russians swear by it. There's Dead Sea salt and mud exfoliation ($55), plus the on-site cafe serves delicious borscht, blintzes and dark bread with smoked fish.

The crowd you'll find here is interesting too: hipsters, older Jews, model types, Europeans and tons of Russian expats. (305-867-8315; www.russianandturkishbaths.com; 5445 Collins Ave; treatments from $40; noon-midnight)

Greeting the Day

Don't miss a sunrise walk along this pretty stretch of Miami Beach. Early morning is a peaceful time to be out, with few people on the sands, and the chance to have those golden, sometimes rose-tinted views to yourself. The lighting can also be pure magic when photographing those iconic lifeguard stations.

Oleta River State Park

STATE PARK

4 MAP P56, C1

Tequesta people were boating the Oleta River estuary as early as 500 BC, so you're following a long tradition if you canoe or kayak in this park. At almost 1000 acres, this is the largest urban park in the state and one of the best places in Miami to escape the madding crowd. Boat out to the local mangrove island, watch the eagles fly by, or just chill on the pretension-free beach.

On-site **ROAM Oleta River Outdoor Center** (📞786-274-7945; https://oletariveroutdoors.com; kayak/canoe rental per 90min $30/45; ⏰9am-6pm Mon-Fri, 8am-7pm Sat & Sun; ♿) rents out kayaks, canoes, stand-up paddleboards and mountain bikes. It also offers paddling tours, yoga classes on stand-up paddleboards and other activities. The park is off 163rd St NE/FL 826 in Sunny Isles, about 8 miles north of North Miami Beach. (📞305-919-1844; www.floridastateparks.org/oletariver; 3400 NE 163rd St; vehicle/pedestrian & bicycle $6/2; ⏰8am-sunset; 🅿♿)

Boardwalk

BEACH

5 MAP P56, C6

Posing is what many people do best in Miami, and there are plenty of skimpily dressed hotties on the Mid-Beach boardwalk, but there are also middle-class Latinos and orthodox Jews, who walk their dogs and play with their kids here, giving the entire place a laid-back, real-world vibe that contrasts with the nonstop glamour of South Beach. (www.miamibeachboardwalk.com; 21st St–46th St)

Haulover Beach Park

PARK

6 MAP P56, C1

Swimsuits are optional at at least part of this 40-acre beach park hidden behind vegetation from the sight of condos, highways and prying passers-by. You don't have to get into your birthday suit if you don't fancy it – in fact, most of the beach is clothed and there's even a dog park. It is one of the nicer spots for sand in the area. It is located on Collins Ave about 4.5 miles north of 71st St. (📞305-947-3525; www.miamidade.gov/parks/haulover.asp; 10800 Collins Ave; per car Mon-Fri $5, Sat & Sun $7; ⏰sunrise-sunset)

Eating

27 Restaurant

FUSION $$

7 MAP P56, C6

Part of Freehand Miami and the very popular bar Broken Shaker (p60), 27 has a lovely setting – akin to dining in an old tropical cottage, with worn floorboards, candlelit tables, and various rooms slung with artwork and curious knickknacks, plus a lovely terrace. Try the braised octopus, crispy pork shoulder, kimchi fried rice and yogurt-tahini-massaged kale.

Book ahead. Brunch is also quite popular. (📞786-476-7020; www.freehandhotels.com; 2727 Indian Creek Dr, Freehand Miami Hotel; mains $17-30; 🕐6-11:30pm Mon-Sat, 11am-3pm Sat & Sun; 🖊)

Cafe Prima Pasta ITALIAN $$

8 ✕ MAP P56, C1

We're not sure what's better at this Argentine-Italian place: the much-touted pasta, which deserves every one of the accolades heaped on it, or the atmosphere, which captures the dignified sultriness of Buenos Aires. You can't go wrong with the small, well-curated menu, with standouts including gnocchi formaggi, baked branzino, and squid-ink linguine with seafood in a lobster sauce. (📞305-867-0106; www.cafeprimapasta.com; 414 71st St;

mains $17-29; 🕐5-11pm Mon-Thu, to 11:30pm Fri & Sat, 4-10:30pm Sun)

Josh's Deli DELI $

9 ✕ MAP P56, D1

Josh's is simplicity itself. Here in the heart of Jewish Miami, you can nosh on thick cuts of house-cured pastrami sandwiches and matzo-ball soup for lunch or challah French toast, eggs and house-cured salmon for breakfast. It's a deliciously authentic slice of Mid-Beach culture. (📞305-397-8494; 9517 Harding Ave; sandwiches $14-18; 🕐8:30am-3:30pm)

Shuckers AMERICAN $$

10 ✕ MAP P56, A2

With excellent views overlooking the waters from the 79th St

Fontainebleau (p57)

Keeping it Kosher in Miami Beach

They are no shtetls, but Arthur Godfrey Rd (41st St) and Harding Ave between 91st and 96th Sts in Surfside are popular thoroughfares for the Jewish population of Miami Beach. Just as the Jewish population have shaped Miami Beach, so has the beach shaped them: you can eat lox *y arroz con moros* (salmon with rice and beans) and while the Orthodox men don yarmulkes and the women wear headscarves, many have nice tans and drive flashy SUVs.

Causeway, Shuckers has to be one of the best-positioned restaurants around. The food is pub grub: burgers, fried fish and the. The chicken wings, basted in several mouthwatering sauces, deep-fried and grilled again, are famous. (☏305-866-1570; www.shuckers barandgrill.com; 1819 79th St Causeway; mains $12-26; ⏰11am-1am; 🛜)

Roasters 'n Toasters
DELI $

11 ✖ MAP P56, C5

Given the crowds and the satisfied smiles of customers, Roasters 'n Toasters meets the demanding standards of Miami Beach's large Jewish demographic, thanks to juicy deli meat, fresh bread, crispy bagels and warm latkes. Sliders (mini-sandwiches) are served on challah bread, an innovation that's as charming as it is tasty. (☏305-531-7691; www.roastersntoasters.com; 525 Arthur Godfrey Rd; mains $10-18; ⏰6am-3:30pm)

Chayhana Oasis
UZBEK $$

12 ✖ MAP P56, D1

Chayhana claims to be an oasis, but with its elaborate tile work and light fixtures, it feels more like a Samarkand palace. A flush and flash Central Asian, Russian and American crowd dine here on steamed dumplings filled with spiced lamb meat, pea soup served with yogurt, *samsa* (traditional savory baked Uzbek pastries) and other Silk Road delights. (☏305-917-1133; http://chayhanaoasis.com; 250 Sunny Isles Blvd; mains $13-34; ⏰noon-11pm)

Drinking

Broken Shaker
BAR

A single small room with a well-equipped bar (see 7 ✖ Map p56, C6) produces expert cocktails, which are mostly consumed in the beautiful, softly lit garden – all of it part of the Freehand Miami hotel. There's a great soundtrack at all times, and the drinks are excellent. The clientele is a mix of hotel guests (young and into partying) and cool locals. (📞305-531-2727; www.freehandhotels.com; 2727 Indian Creek Dr, ⏱5:30pm-2am Mon-Thu, 4:30pm-3am Fri, 1pm-3am Sat, to 2am Sun)

Bob's Your Uncle
BAR

13 🌐 MAP P56, C1

Bob's Your Uncle's name doesn't just derive from the saying. 'Bob' is simple, and so is this bar: classic cocktails, good beer, spacious seating, old games, friendly service, and the chillest vibe in Miami Beach. It's just a decently priced spot where you can grab a drink and catch up with friends, and that's something beautiful. (📞786-542-5366; www.bobsyourunclemiami.com; 928 71st St; ⏱3pm-3am)

On The Rocks
SPORTS BAR

14 🌐 MAP P56, D1

This convivial neighborhood dive feels pulled from another era, a feeling underlined by the multiple racks of old liquor bottles behind the bar and the nicely faded feel of the whole establishment. Grab a cold beer, watch the game with locals on either side of you, and relax. (📞305-864-2444; https://ontherocksmiamibeach.com; 217 71st St; ⏱8am-5am)

Entertainment

North Beach Bandshell
LIVE MUSIC

15 ⭐ MAP P56, D1

This outdoor venue features an excellent lineup of concerts, dance, theater, opera and spoken word throughout the year. Some events are free. It's run by the nonprofit Rhythm Foundation, and the wide-ranging repertoire features sounds from around the globe, with many family-friendly events. Check online to see what's on the roster. (📞786-453-2897; www.northbeachbandshell.com; 7275 Collins Ave)

Walking Tour 🚶

Surprises of the Upper East Side

Northeast of Wynwood, the Upper East Side is stuffed with creative shops, art studios and cafes, many of which have opened in the past few years. There are plenty of pleasant surprises here, from a great Eastern European market to kayaking spots on the bay.

Getting There

🚌 Several buses run along Biscayne Blvd, including routes 3, 16 and 93, which you can catch on 29th St near Wynwood. From Downtown, take bus 93. From Mid-Beach, take bus 112.

❶ Morningside Park

Located on the waterfront, this aptly named **park** (750 NE 55th Tce) is a great spot in the morning, when the golden light is just right. On Saturdays, you can hire kayaks (from $12 per hour) and stand-up paddleboards (from $20 per hour).

❷ New Yorker

This **hotel** (www.hotelnewyorker miami.com; 6500 Biscayne Blvd), with its frosty white walls and vintage neon, looks MiMo (Miami Modern) enough to star in a Tarantino movie. Speaking of which, the patio bar is a perfect spot for people watching a fascinating selection of Miami creative types.

❸ Legion Park Farmers Market

For a taste of local culture, stop by this small **farmers market** (cnr Biscayne Blvd & 66th St, Legion Park; ◷9am-2pm Sat) held each Saturday in the Upper East Side's Legion Park. The local crowd is a cross section of the new Upper East Side: a blend of bohemian types and young families.

❹ Vagabond Hotel

An icon in the MiMo district, the Vagabond is a 1953 motel and restaurant where Frank Sinatra and other Rat Packers used to hang out. Today it's been reborn as a boutique hotel, has lost none of its allure and has a great **bar** (☎305-400-8420; www.thevagabond hotelmiami.com; 7301 Biscayne Blvd; ◷5pm-midnight Mon-Fri, from noon Sat & Sun).

❺ Miami Ironside

Ironside (☎305-438-9002; www. miamiironside.com; 7610 NE 4th Ct; 🚴🏃) is a pleasant hub of creativity where you'll find art and design studios, showrooms and galleries as well as a few eating and drinking spaces. It's a lushly landscaped property, with some intriguing public art.

❻ Marky's Gourmet

A Miami institution among Russians, Russophiles and those who simply love to explore global cuisine, **Marky's** (☎305-758-9288; www. markys.com; 687 NE 79th St; ◷9am-7pm Mon-Wed, to 9pm Thu-Sat, 10am-5pm Sun) has been going strong since 1983. In-the-know foodies from afar flock here to load up on gourmet cheeses, olives, European-style sausages, wines, cakes, teas, jams, chocolates and caviar.

❼ The Anderson

The Anderson (☎786-401-6330; www.theandersonmiami.com; 709 NE 79th St; ◷5pm-2am Sun-Thu, to 4am Fri & Sat) is a great bar with a dimly lit interior sprinkled with red couches, animal-print fabrics, wild wallpaper and lots of 1980s affections. Head to the back patio for a tropical-themed setting where you can dip your toes in the sand (absent an actual oceanfront).

Explore
Downtown Miami

Downtown Miami, the city's international financial and banking center, is a contrast of tatty indoor shopping arcades filled with takeout spots and cheap electronics outlets, high-rise luxury hotels, condos, cultural institutions and flash retail spaces, particularly around the Brickell neighborhood. At night, the towers are illuminated in hot pinks and cool blues – the effect is unmistakably magical.

The Short List

○ **Pérez Art Museum Miami (p66)** *Checking out the latest contemporary show and wandering the waterfront sculpture garden.*

○ **Adrienne Arsht Center for the Performing Arts (p68)** *Taking a free behind-the-scenes tour, then returning for an evening concert.*

○ **Bayfront Park (p70)** *Relaxing on the grass to a panorama of Biscayne Bay.*

○ **HistoryMiami (p76)** *Learning the tales of Miami's early days at this historical museum.*

○ **Patricia & Phillip Frost Museum of Science (p76)** *Marveling all things great and small with kids.*

Getting There & Around

M Miami's free Metromover monorail is useful for getting around Downtown.

🚃 Several trolleys connect Downtown with points north and south.

🚲 Citi Bike has many stations here.

⚓ Water Taxi Miami provides ferry transport between South Beach and Bayside Marketplace.

Downtown Miami Map on p74

Brickell Avenue Bridge (p73) SEAN PAVONE/SHUTTERSTOCK©

Top Sight 📷
Pérez Art Museum Miami

Miami has no shortage of first-rate galleries and intriguing museums. The Pérez, though, is in a category of its own. This gorgeous building, designed by Pritzker Prize–winning architecture firm Herzog & de Meuron, houses world-class contemporary art. And the collection looks all the more impressive viewed in these light-filled galleries on the edge of Biscayne Bay.

◉ MAP P74, E2

☏ 305-375-3000

www.pamm.org

1103 Biscayne Blvd

adult/senior & student $16/12, 1st Thu & 2nd Sat of month free

🕐 10am-6pm Fri-Tue, to 9pm Thu

The Architecture

Swiss architects Herzog & de Meuron designed this 200,000-sq-ft space, which opened to much fanfare in 2013. The three-story building sits on an elevated platform that gives it fine views over the water and the grassy park abutting it. The views play a supporting role both in the museum galleries and in the restaurant, which fronts a particularly scenic stretch of bay.

The building also mimics elements of the South Florida landscape – the many slender columns under the canopy on the back terrace, for instance, can be read as a kind of mangrove system, with its many roots extending out.

One of the most striking features of the building is its hanging gardens, the long columnlike tubes dangling from the rooftop. Each one is bursting with plants. Dozens of plant species – all native to the region – are nourished by rainwater fed through concealed irrigation tubes within the columns.

Even the parking lot spurns convention. It lies beneath the museum and is open to the sides, with shrubs and greenery surrounding it. It has a pebble-lined floor rather than pavement, which maintains a more fluid connection to the landscape.

The Experience

The permanent collection, typically exhibited on the ground floor, rotates through unique pieces every few months. The temporary shows and retrospectives by artists such as Ai Weiwei, Julio Le Parc and Robert Rauschenberg are the star attraction for many locals.

The designers of the museum wanted to create a place that all Miami residents feel they have access to. You can come and hang out in the grassy park, or sit on the steps or the deck chairs enjoying the views over the water.

★ **Top Tips**

○ Take advantage of free admission days. PAMM is free on the first Thursday and the second Saturday of the month.

○ Museum guides lead excellent, free 45-minute tours daily (except Wednesday) at noon and 2:30pm, as well as 6:30pm Thursday.

○ Check the online calendar for upcoming film screenings, gallery talks and art-making workshops.

✕ **Take a Break**

Stop by Verde (p79) for salads, sandwiches, drinks and fine views.

A 10-minute walk from the museum, All Day (p78) is great for coffee and light fare.

Downtown Miami Pérez Art Museum Miami

Top Sight 📷

Adrienne Arsht Center for the Performing Arts

New York has the Lincoln Center, Sydney has its Opera House and Miami has the Adrienne Arsht Center, a much-loved performing arts hall, where you can see some of the world's top ballets, musical soloists and theatrical productions.

◎ MAP P74, D2

📞 305-949-6722

www.arshtcenter.org

1300 Biscayne Blvd

🕑 box office noon-5pm Mon-Fri, plus 2hr before performances

The Design

The Arsht Center comprises three separate venues. The biggest hall is found in the Ziff Ballet Opera House, a 2400-seat venue that stages ballets, musicals, Broadway shows and of course, opera. It has a massive stage – the second-largest in the country – and can accommodate up to 1000 people. Across Biscayne Blvd is the Knight Concert Hall. This 2200-seat, three-tiered theater is for musical concerts and has superb acoustics. The smallest venue is the 300-seat Carnival Studio Theater, a flexible black-box space located inside the Ziff Ballet Opera House.

The Ziff Ballet Opera House is centered on a horseshoe-shaped design that gives excellent views no matter where you sit. The ceiling has a round acoustical dome with a nautilus-like swirl, ringed by a halo of tiny pinpricks of lights. Upon entering, you may notice a remarkable work of art: a long white hand extending out in a gesture of welcome, surrounded by stars, vocalizing figureheads and abstract forms. The hand has its counterpart, featured in black, over in the Knight Concert Hall.

On the acoustic front, this place is basically a box within a box within a box. No outside sounds – whether roaring jet engines overhead, or the everyday traffic right outside – can penetrate.

The Location

Up on the second and third floors of the Ziff, you can gaze through the floor-to-ceiling windows over the skyscraper canyons of Downtown Miami – a vista all the more remarkable when you consider many buildings on view weren't here a decade ago. The Arsht Center was one of the first big arrivals to Downtown and many locals thought the planners were crazy to build where they did. Now it's the nexus of a growing arts complex.

★ **Top Tips**

○ Free guided tours are offered at noon on Mondays and Saturdays. Call ahead to check they're running.

○ Buy tickets online or via the box office (open 10am to 6pm Monday to Friday, and noon until curtain time when there's a show on Saturday and Sunday).

✕ **Take a Break**

Book a pre-performance meal at **Brava by Brad Kilgore** (☎786-468-2365; www.bravaby bradkilgore.com; mains $31-44; ⏱5:30-9pm on show nights), known for creative French food.

On show days, the Cafe at Books & Books (p79) serves a prix-fixe menu of local and sustainable fare. Reserve ahead.

Top Sight 📷
Bayfront Park

Folks from all walks of life flock to this green oasis on the edge of Downtown Miami. Aside from marvelous views over the water, this is the place for leisurely strolls, picnics on the grass, open-air concerts, free yoga sessions and even high-flying trapeze classes.

◎ MAP P74, E5

☎ 305-358-7550

www.bayfrontparkmiami.com

301 N Biscayne Blvd

Concerts & Big Events

Throughout the year, Bayfront Park hosts a mix of big and small events, including one of South Florida's best fireworks shows, the Independence Day pyrotechnics that fill the night sky on July 4th.

Near the center of the park is the **Klipsch Amphitheater** (www.klipsch.com/klipsch-amphi theater-at-bayfront-park), which boasts excellent views over Biscayne Bay. It's a good spot for live-music shows, with seating for 7500. Occasionally top names give free concerts; Jennifer Lopez has performed here in recent years.

Noguchi Sculptures

Renowned artist and landscape architect Isamu Noguchi redesigned much of the 32-acre Bayfront Park in the 1980s, and dotted the grounds with three of his own sculptures (one of which is pictured, left). The **Light Tower** is a 40ft, somewhat abstract allusion to Japanese lanterns and moonlight over Miami.

In the southwest corner of the park is the **Challenger Memorial**, a monument designed for the astronauts killed in the 1986 space-shuttle explosion. It was built to resemble both the twisting helix of a human DNA chain and the shuttle itself.

Slide Mantra is a twisting spiral of Carrara marble that doubles as a playground piece for the kids – Noguchi believed that children could gain a new appreciation of sculpture through play.

Yoga in the Park

The Tina Hills Pavilion, at the south end of the park, is also the setting for free open-air **yoga classes** (www.bayfrontparkmiami.com/YogaClasses. html; ⏱6pm Mon-Thu, 9am Sat), suitable for all levels. It's quite a sight seeing dozens (sometimes up to 100) people moving together against a sweeping backdrop of skyscrapers and the grassy, tree-dotted landscape with the sparkling waters just beyond.

★ **Top Tips**

◦ Head to the park in the late afternoon and watch the skyscrapers of Downtown light up as the sun goes down.

◦ Tack on a stroll along the nearby Miami Riverwalk for more great waterfront views.

◦ Time your visit to catch an outdoor concert or a free yoga class.

✕ **Take a Break**

◦ Stroll a few blocks west to CVI.CHE 105 (p81) for excellent Peruvian fare.

◦ Nearby Manna Life Food (p73) is a healthy, ecofriendly snack spot.

Walking Tour 🥾

Stroll Through Downtown & Brickell

Downtown Miami is constantly reinventing itself via construction and early adoption of whatever the world thinks is cool. If you want to have your finger on the pulse of what's on trend, this walk will lead you past the shiniest corners inhabited by Miami's relentlessly cool kids.

Walk Facts

Start Manna Life Food

End Sugar

Length 2.4 miles; three to four hours

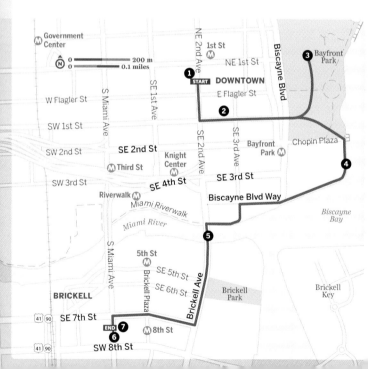

❶ Manna Life Food

This airy, stylish **eatery** (www.mannalifefood.com; 80 NE 2nd Ave; mains $8-12; ⏱10am-6pm Mon-Fri, 11am-4pm Sat) has wowed diners with its plant-based menu, which offers superfood ingredients like red quinoa, baked tofu, roasted veggies, coconut brown rice and raw falafel. It's also a good spot for fresh juices, coffees and matcha cappuccinos.

❷ Supply & Advise

Supply & Advise (p83) is where male travelers want to head if they're looking to get looked at. There's a ton of handsome clothing, which is housed in a historic building that dates to the 1920s. Do clothes make the man? Not at all, which is why there's a pretty sweet barber shop here as well.

❸ Bayfront Park

Few American parks can claim to front such a lovely stretch of bright turquoise (Biscayne Bay), but Miamians are lucky like that. This long expanse (p70) that backs onto Downtown is a great spot for leisurely waterside walks, picnics and outdoor concerts

❹ Miami Riverwalk

This pedestrian walkway follows along the northern edge of the river as it bisects Downtown, and offers some peaceful vantage points of bridges and skyscrapers dotting the urban landscape. You can start the walk at the south end of Bayfront Park and follow it under bridges and along the waterline until it ends just west of the SW 2nd Ave Bridge.

❺ Brickell Avenue Bridge

Crossing the Miami River, the lovely Brickell Avenue Bridge between SE 4th St and SE 5th St was made wider and higher some years back, affording even better views of the Downtown skyline. Note the 17ft bronze statue by Cuban-born sculptor Manuel Carbonell of a Tequesta Indian warrior and his family, which sits atop the towering Pillar of History column.

❻ Brickell City Centre

There's much to entice both Miami residents and visitors to this **center** (www.brickellcitycentre.com; 701 S Miami Ave; ⏱10am-9:30pm Mon-Sat, noon-7pm Sun), with restaurants, bars, a cinema and loads of high-end retailers (Ted Baker, All Saints, Kendra Scott). You'll find shops scattered across both sides of S Miami Ave between 7th and 8th Sts, including a massive Saks Fifth Ave.

❼ Sugar

One of Miami's hottest bars, **Sugar** (www.east-miami.com/en/restaurants-and-bars/sugar; 788 Brickell Plaza, EAST, Miami Hotel, 40th fl; ⏱noon-1am Sun-Wed, to 3am Thu-Sat) sits on the 40th floor of the EAST Miami Hotel. Calling it a rooftop bar doesn't quite do the place justice. Verdant oasis is more like it, with an open-air deck, plants and trees, and sweeping views over the Key Biscayne.

74

Downtown Miami

F
NE 15th St
Herald Plaza

E
Adrienne
Arsht
Center
Biscayne Blvd

D
NE 2nd Ave
School
Board
NE 14th St
NE 15th St

C
N Miami Ave
NE 16th St
22

B
NW 1st Ave
500 m
0.25 miles
NW 3rd Ave
NW 3rd Ave

A
N

1
5

2
Biscayne Bay
Pérez Art
Museum Miami
10
Museum Park
Patricia & Phillip Frost 2
Museum of Science
Museum Park
25
27
Adrienne Arsht Center
for the Performing Arts
NE 13th St
NE 12th St
NE 13th St
11th St
NE 2nd Ave
20
18
8
NE 10th St
DOWNTOWN
N Miami Ave
NW 1st Ave
Overtown
NW 1st Ct
Metrorail
NW 2nd Ave
North-South Expwy

3
Port Blvd
Museum Park
23
Freedom
Tower
3
MDC Museum
of Art & Design
College
North
NE 4th St
NE 5th St
NE 6th St
NE 7th St
NE 8th St
NE 9th St
Park
West
Wilkie D
Ferguson Jr
6
MiamiCentral
NW 1st Ave

4
Marina
Bayside
Marketplace
NW 3rd Ct
NW 4th Ave
NW 5th St
NW 6th St
NW 8th St
NW 9th St
NW 10th St

Downtown Miami

For reviews see

⊙	Top Sights	p66
⊙	Sights	p76
⊗	Eating	p77
⊗	Drinking	p81
⊗	Entertainment	p82
ⓜ	Shopping	p83

Biscayne Bay

Bayfront Park ⊙

Biscayne Blvd

Miami Center for Architecture & Design ⊙ 4

Chopin Plaza

College/ Bayside

⊗12

⊗7

⊗14

⊗15

⊙21

Bayfront Park Ⓜ

NE 3rd St

NE 2nd St

NE 2nd Ave

1st St

⊙17

⊙24

29 ⓜ

Knight Center

Ⓜ

SE 3rd St

Biscayne Blvd Way

Brickell Ave Bridge

Brickell Park

Brickell Key Dr

E Flagler St

SE 1st St

SE 2nd St

Ⓜ Third St

SE 4th St

Ⓜ Riverwalk

Miami River

5th St Ⓜ

SE 5th St

⊗19

SE 6th St

Brickell Ave

⊙8th St

S Miami Ave

W Flagler St

SW 2nd St

DOWNTOWN

Miami River Bridges

Metrorail

⊗9

S Miami Ave

⊙16

⊗11

SW 1st Ave

SW 9th St

⊙28 ⓜ

Government Center Ⓜ

History Miami ⊙1

Government Center

SW 1st St

41 90

41 90

BRICKELL

NW 3rd St

NW 2nd St

Lummus Park

NW North River Dr

Miami River

José Martí Riverfront Park

968

968

SW 4th Ave

SW 3rd Ave

SW 1st St

W Flagler St

SW 7th St

SW 8th St (Calle Ocho)

SW 3rd Ave

SW 9th St

NW 4th St

⊗13

⊙26

SW 4th Ave

SW 5th Ave

SW 2nd St

SW 3rd St

SW 5th St

SW 6th St

SW 7th St

Sights

HistoryMiami
MUSEUM

1 ◉ MAP P74, C6

South Florida – a land of escaped slaves, guerrilla Native Americans, gangsters, land grabbers, pirates, tourists, drug dealers and alligators – has a special history, and it takes a special kind of museum to capture that narrative. This highly recommended place, located in the Miami-Dade Cultural Center, does just that, weaving together the stories of the region's successive waves of population, from Native Americans to Nicaraguans. (☏305-375-1492; www.historymiami. org; 101 W Flagler St; adult/child 6-12yr $10/5; ⏱10am-5pm Tue-Sat, from noon Sun; ⛹)

Patricia & Phillip Frost Museum of Science
MUSEUM

2 ◉ MAP P74, E2

This sprawling new Downtown museum spreads across 250,000 sq ft that includes a three-level aquarium, a 250-seat state-of-the-art planetarium, and two distinct wings that delve into the wonders of science and nature. Exhibitions range from weather phenomena to creepy crawlies, feathered dinosaurs and vital microbe displays, while Florida's fascinating Everglades and biologically rich coral reefs play starring roles. (☏305-434-9600; www.frostscience. org; 1101 Biscayne Blvd; adult/child $25/22; ⏱9:30am-6pm; P ⛹)

MDC Museum of Art & Design
MUSEUM

3 ◉ MAP P74, D4

Miami-Dade College operates a small but well-curated art museum in Downtown; the permanent collection includes works by Matisse, Picasso and Chagall and focuses on minimalism, pop art and contemporary Latin American art. The museum's home building is art itself: it's set in the soaring 255ft (78m) **Freedom Tower** (⏱10am-5pm), a masterpiece of Mediterranean Revival, built in 1925. (☏305-237-7700; www.mdcmoad. org; 600 Biscayne Blvd; adult/student $12/5; ⏱1-6pm Wed & Fri-Sun, to 8pm Thu)

Miami Center for Architecture & Design
MUSEUM

4 ◉ MAP P74, E6

The Miami branch of the American Institute of Architects shares a building with the Downtown Miami Welcome Center. MCAD houses lectures and events related to architecture, design and urban planning, and hosts temporary exhibitions on all of the above subjects. Two-hour walking tours on alternate Saturdays depart from here (at 10am), and take in some of the historic buildings of Downtown. Visit the website for upcoming times and reservations. (Old US Post Office; ☏305-448-7488; www.miamicad. org; 310 SE 1st St; admission free; ⏱10am-5pm Mon-Fri)

Miami Children's Museum
MUSEUM

5 ⊙ MAP P74, F2

This museum, located between South Beach and Downtown Miami, is a bit like an uber-playhouse, with areas for kids to practice all sorts of adult activities – banking and food shopping, caring for pets, and acting as a local cop or firefighter. Adults must go accompanied by children, and vice versa. (📞305-373-5437; www.miamichildrens museum.org; 980 MacArthur Causeway; $22; ⊙10am-6pm; P 🚼)

MiamiCentral
NOTABLE BUILDING

6 ⊙ MAP P74, C4

This train station has been converted into a 9-acre mixed-use complex that houses a food hall, shopping arcades, plus office and residential space. Architecturally, it's like the space age has landed in South Florida, an unmissable jumble of odd angles, enormous windows and twisted steel, designed by Skidmore, Owings & Merrill, the firm responsible for Dubai's Burj Khalifa. The station will be the Miami home of Brightline trains. (Virgin MiamiCentral; https://virgin miamicentral.com; NW 1st Ave, btwn NW 3rd St & NW 8th St; admission free; 🚇Government Center)

Eating

NIU Kitchen
SPANISH $$

7 🍴 MAP P74, D5

NIU is a stylish living-room-sized restaurant serving delectable contemporary Catalan cuisine. It's

Patricia & Phillip Frost Museum of Science

Miami
Critical Mass

If you're in Miami at the beginning of the weekend late in any given month, you may spot hordes of cyclists and, less frequently, some skateboarders, roller-skaters and other self-propelled individuals. So what's it all about?

It's Miami Critical Mass. The event is meant to raise awareness of cycling and indirectly advocate for increased bicycle infrastructure in the city. Anyone is welcome to join; the mass ride gathers at Government Center by HistoryMiami (p76) on the last Friday of each month.

The event is loosely organized, but you can usually find information on it at www.themiamibikescene.com. Generally, the riders gather around 6:30pm, before departing on the 12-to-18-mile trek at 7:15pm. The average speed of the ride is a not-too-taxing 12mph, and you will be expected to keep up (at the same time, you're not to go faster than the pacesetters). All in all it's a fun experience, and a good way to meet members of the local cycling community.

a showcase of culinary pyrotechnics, featuring imaginative sharing plates like Ous (poached eggs, truffled potato foam, *jamón ibérico* and black truffle) or Toninya (smoked tuna, green *guindillas* and pine nuts). The wine list is excellent. (☑786-542-5070; www.niukitchen.com; 134 NE 2nd Ave; sharing plates $14-26; ⊘noon-3:30pm & 6-10pm Mon-Thu, to 11pm Fri, 1-4pm & 6-11pm Sat, 6-10pm Sun; ☑)

All Day   CAFE $

8 MAP P74, C3

All Day is positively Miami's best cafe – with locally sourced ingredients forming the basis of its simple menu, as well as excellent coffees, teas, beer and wine, and an airy, light Scandinavian-style decor, this is a winner all-around.

Stylish chairs, wood-and-marble tables, friendly staff and an always enticing soundtrack lend it an easygoing vibe.

Featuring ingredients sourced from small Florida farms, the cooking is first rate: cast-iron skillet fried eggs with thick sourdough toast, housemade pastrami, smoked-mahi tartines (open-faced sandwich) and tender baby-kale salads. Outstanding coffees and pastries too, and you can also have beer and wine. (☑305-699-3447; www.alldaymia.com; 1035 N Miami Ave; coffee from $3.50, breakfast $10-19; ⊘7am-5pm Mon-Fri, from 9am Sat & Sun; �)

River Oyster Bar   SEAFOOD $$

9 MAP P74, C8

A few paces from the Miami River, this buzzing little spot with a classy vibe whips up excellent plates of seafood. Start off with their fresh showcase oysters and ceviche before moving on to grilled red snapper or yellowfin tuna. For a decadent meal, go for a grand seafood platter ($125), piled high with Neptune's culinary treasures.

Come for lunch for multi-course meals for $20, or at happy hour (4:30pm to 7pm) for appetizer and drinking deals. Reservations are essential. (📞305-530-1915; www.therivermiami.com; 650 S Miami Ave; mains $12-40; 🕙noon-10:30pm Sun-Thu, to midnight Fri & Sat)

Verde
AMERICAN $$

10 🏴 MAP P74, E2

Inside the Pérez Art Museum Miami (p66), Verde is a local favorite for its tasty market-fresh dishes and great setting – with outdoor seating on a terrace overlooking the bay. Crispy *mahi-mahi* (dorado fish) tacos, pizza with squash blossoms and goat cheese, and grilled endive salads are among the temptations. (📞786-345-5697; www.pamm.org/dining; 1103 Biscayne Blvd; mains $15-25; 🕙11am-4pm Mon, Tue & Fri, to 9pm Thu, to 5pm Sat & Sun; 🅿)

Cafe at Books & Books
BISTRO $$

During shows at the Adrienne Arsht Center, reserve ahead for a two- or three-course meal of nicely turned out plates of pan-seared *mahi-mahi* or rosemary roasted chicken breast with ancient grains with vegetables. At other times, this handsomely set eatery (see **27** 🅰 Map p74, D2) serves à la carte, with similar dishes on offer. (📞786-405-1745; www.arshtcenter.org/visit/cafe-books-books; 1300 Biscayne Blvd, Adrienne Arsht Center for the Performing Arts; prix-fixe menu $35-40, mains $14-25; 🕙11am-8pm; 🅿)

La Moon
COLOMBIAN $

11 🏴 MAP P74, C8

Nothing hits the spot after a late night of partying quite like red beans, rice, sausage, pork belly and plantains, or sweet corn cakes stuffed with steak. These street-food delicacies are available well into the wee hours on weekend nights, plus La Moon is conveniently located within stumbling distance of bars including Blackbird Ordinary (p81). Top it off with a *refajo*: Colombian beer (Aguila) with Colombian soda (preferably the red one). (📞305-860-6209; www.lamoonrestaurant.com; 97 SW 8th St; mains $7-17; 🕙11am-midnight Sun & Tue-Thu, to 6am Fri & Sat)

Bali Cafe
INDONESIAN $

12 🏴 MAP P74, D5

It's odd to think of the clean flavors of sushi and the bright richness of Indonesian cuisine coming together in harmony, but they're happily married in this tropical hole-in-the-wall. Have some spicy tuna rolls for an appetizer, then follow up with *soto betawi* – beef soup cooked with coconut milk, ginger and shallots. (📞305-358-5751; 109 NE 2nd

Miami's Public Art

This city has always been way ahead of the curve when it comes to public art. Miami and Miami Beach established the Art in Public Places program back in 1973, when it voted to allocate 1.5% of city construction funds to the fostering of public art. Since then more than 700 works – sculptures, mosaics, murals, light-based installations and more – have been created in public spots.

Barbara Neijna's *Foreverglades,* in Concourse J of Miami International Airport, uses mosaic, art-installed text from *River of Grass* (by Marjory Stoneman Douglas) and waves representing the movement of water over grass to give new arrivals a sense of the flow of Florida's unique ecosystem. A series of handprints representing Miami's many immigrant communities link into a single community in *Reaching for Miami Skies,* by Connie Lloveras, which greets Metromover commuters at Brickell Station. In Miami-Dade Library, the floating text of *Words Without Thought Never to Heaven Go* by Edward Ruscha challenges readers to engage in thought processes that are inspired by, but go beyond, the books that surround them. The team of Roberto Behar and Rosario Marquardt, hailing from Argentina, have been among the most prolific public artists in town, to the degree that their work is deliberately meant to warp conceptions of what is or isn't public space; they created the giant red *M* at the Metromover Riverwalk Station for the city's centennial back in 1996. Japanese-American artist Isamu Noguchi designed Bayfront Park in 1986, which is also where you can see Noguchi's 'Slide Mantra', a Carrera marble sculpture that's both playful and meditative.

Ave; mains $10-15; ⊙11am-4pm daily, 6-10pm Mon-Fri; 🥢)

Casablanca
SEAFOOD $$

13 🍴 MAP P74, A5

Perched over the Miami River, Casablanca serves excellent seafood. The setting is a big draw – with tables on a long wooden deck just above the water, and the odd seagull winging past. But the fresh fish is the real star here.

Start off with oysters (half price all day on Wednesdays) or grilled octopus, before moving on to a sizzling *parrillada* (grilled platter) piled high with prawns, calamari, oysters, clams and grilled fish. Casablanca's fish market is right next door. (📞305-371-4107; www.casablancaseafood.com; 400 NW North River Dr; mains $14-40; ⊙11am-10pm Mon-Thu, to 11pm Fri, 7am-10pm Sat & Sun)

Soya e Pomodoro
ITALIAN $$

14 ⊗ MAP P74, D5

Soya e Pomodoro feels like a bohemian retreat for Italian artists and filmmakers, who can dine on bowls of fresh pasta under vintage posters, rainbow paintings and curious wall-hangings. Adding to the vibe is live Latin jazz (on Thursday nights from 9pm to midnight), plus readings and other arts events that take place here on select evenings. (✆305-381-9511; www.soyae pomodoro.com; 120 NE 1st St; lunch $10-19, dinner $13-29; ⊙11:30am-4:30pm Mon-Fri, 7-11:30pm Wed-Sat)

CVI.CHE 105
PERUVIAN $$

15 ⊗ MAP P74, E5

White is the design element of choice in Juan Chipoco's ever-popular Peruvian Downtown eatery. Beautifully presented ceviches, *lomo saltado* (marinated steak) and *arroz con mariscos* (seafood rice) are ideal for sharing and go down nicely with a round of Pisco Fuegos (made with jalapeño-infused pisco) and other specialty Peruvian cocktails. (✆305-577-3454; www.ceviche105.com; 105 NE 3rd Ave; ma$12-30; ⊙noon-10pm Sun-Thu, to 11pm Fri & Sat)

Drinking

Blackbird Ordinary
BAR

16 ⊙ MAP P74, C8

The Blackbird is an excellent bar, with great cocktails and a vibe that manages to strike a good balance between laid back and Miami hedonism. The only thing 'ordinary' about the place is the sense that all are welcome for a fun and pretension-free night out. You can often catch great live music, and on quiet nights there's always a pool table. (✆305-671-3307; www. blackbirdordinary.com; 729 SW 1st Ave; ⊙3pm-5am Mon-Fri, from 5pm Sat & Sun)

Lost Boy
BAR

17 ⊙ MAP P74, D6

Miami is a city full of impressive looking bars, but few pull off vintage aesthetics like Lost Boy, which makes sense, as it is housed in one of the oldest-standing buildings in Downtown. Vintage Cuban furniture, brass knobs, exposed brick and lots of old wood come together into an enormous pub with straightforward cocktails and beers served in Imperial pint glasses. (✆305-372-7303; www. lostboydrygoods.com; 157 E Flagler St; ⊙noon-2am Mon-Sat, to midnight Sun)

The Corner
BAR

18 ⊙ MAP P74, C3

This excellent bar sits near ELEVEN, which is ironic as the Corner couldn't have a more different vibe. The interior, all dark wood and dim lighting, looks like it could double as a fancy old British library. Many folks still choose to drink outdoors – this is Miami, after all –sipping classic cocktails and cold beers.

It attracts a non-fussy, creative professional crowd. (📞305-961-7887; www.thecornermiami.com; 1035 N Miami Ave; ⏰4pm-5am Sun-Thu, to 8am Fri & Sat)

Baby Jane
BAR

19 MAP P74, D7

Small but sexy, Baby Jane is a Brickell outpost filled with tropical accents, neon, and Pacific Rim meets the Caribbean cocktails like the Big Trouble in Little Havana, which features *flor de caña* rum infused with wontons, a sentence we could only write in Miami. The crowd seems to mainly be downtown cool kids, but the vibe is laid back. (📞786-623-3555; www.babyjanemiami.com; 500 Brickell Ave; ⏰noon-3am Sun-Thu, to 5am Fri & Sat)

Eleven Miami
CLUB

20 🍸 MAP P74, C2

Since its opening way back in 2014, Eleven Miami has remained one of the top Downtown clubs. There's much eye candy here (and we're not talking just about the attractive club-goers): go-go dancers, aerialists and racy (striptease-esque) performances, amid a state-of-the-art sound system, laser lights and video walls, with top DJs working the crowd into a frenzy. The space (20,000 sq ft) is massive with a sizeable roof deck, and it never closes its doors. (📞786-460-4803; www.11miami.com; 29 NE 11th St; ⏰24hr)

Mama Tried
BAR

21 🍸 MAP P74, D5

She really did. And she pulled off a very fine bar here in the heart of Downtown. Look for an orange neon sign, then walk into a dark bar with a speakeasy feel, giant metallic light fixtures, and a big square bar. It's got a laid-back, even neighborhood vibe on week-days, but turns into an absolute Miami dance party on weekend nights. (http://mamatriedmia.com; 207 NE 1st St; ⏰3pm-5am Mon-Fri, from 5pm Sat & Sun)

Esotico
COCKTAIL BAR

22 🍸 MAP P74, D1

Who knew there was a jungle in the middle of Downtown Miami? That's the sense one gets after walking into Esotico, all leafy plants, green murals and hot neon. Tiki drinks are as sultry as the set-ting, ranging from Zombies to new spins on the Colada. A breakfast cocktail of rum, ginger syrup, lime juice and bananas is flat out stunning. (📞305-800-8454; www.esoticomiami.com; 1600 NE 1st Ave; ⏰5pm-1am Mon-Thu, to 2am Fri & Sat)

Entertainment

American Airlines Arena
STADIUM

23 MAP P74, E4

Resembling a massive spaceship that perpetually hovers at the edge of Biscayne Bay, this arena has been the home of the city's NBA franchise, the Miami Heat, since 2000. The Waterfront Theater, Florida's largest, is housed inside; throughout the year it hosts concerts, Broadway performances and the like. (786-777-1000; www. aaarena.com; 601 N Biscayne Blvd)

Olympia Theater PERFORMING ARTS

24 MAP P74, D6

This elegantly renovated 1920s movie palace services a huge variety of performing arts including film festivals, symphonies, ballets and touring shows. The acoustics are excellent. (305-374-2444; www. olympiatheater.org; 174 E Flagler St)

Florida Grand Opera OPERA

25 MAP P74, D2

Founded in the 1940s, this highly respected opera company, which stages many shows including *Madame Butterfly*, *La Bohème* and *Tosca*, performs throughout the year at the Adrienne Arsht Center for the Performing Arts and in Fort Lauderdale. (800-741-1010; www. fgo.org; 1300 Biscayne Blvd, Adrienne Arsht Center for the Performing Arts)

Miami Hispanic Cultural Arts Center DANCE

26 MAP P74, A6

Directed by Cuban-trained Pedro Pablo Peña, this troupe presents mainly classical ballets based out of a lovely venue also known as 'The White House of Ballet.' (786-747-1877; www.miamihispanicballet. org; 111 SW 5th Ave)

Shopping

Books & Books BOOKS

27 MAP P74, D2

This excellent bookstore has a small branch in the Adrienne Arsht Center for the Performing Arts, which includes a lovely open-air cafe (p79). (786-405-1744; 1300 Biscayne Blvd, Adrienne Arsht Center for the Performing Arts; 11:30am-8pm)

Mary Brickell Village SHOPPING CENTER

28 MAP P74, C8

This outdoor shopping and dining complex has helped revitalize the Brickell neighborhood, with a range of boutiques, restaurants, cafes and bars. It's a magnet for new condo residents in the area, with a central location in the heart of the financial district. (305-381-6130; www.marybrickellvillage. com; 901 S Miami Ave; 10am-9pm Mon-Sat, noon-6pm Sun)

Supply & Advise CLOTHING

29 MAP P74, D6

Supply & Advise brings a heavy dose of men's fashion to Down-town Miami, with rugged, well-made and handsomely tailored clothing, plus shoes and accesso-ries, set in a historic 1920s build-ing. There's also a barbershop, complete with vintage chairs and that impeccable look of bygone days. (305-960-2043; www. supplyandadvise.com; 223 SE 1st St; 11am-7pm Mon-Sat)

Downtown Miami Shopping

Explore ◈
Wynwood & the Design District

Wynwood is Miami's hippest neighborhood, and it knows it. This is an adult playground of graffiti, murals, restaurants, bars, shops and galleries. Whatever is cool and on trend in the world is emulated, if not started, on these streets, in the shadow of some excellent public art. The Design District is a high-end shopping area, where the line between neighborhood and mall is tough to draw.

The Short List

○ **Wynwood Walls (p86)** *Checking out the stunning outdoor murals at the epicenter of Wynwood.*

○ **Margulies Collection at the Warehouse (p94)** *Exploring thought-provoking works by some of the world's top contemporary artists.*

○ **De La Cruz Collection (p91)** *Perusing paintings and sculptures from Latin America and Europe.*

○ **Wynwood Marketplace (p94)** *Relaxing, dining and enjoying this open air, daily street festival.*

○ **NW 2nd Ave (p101)** *Browsing one-of-a-kind clothing and curio shops, like Malaquita, along this major shopping corridor.*

Getting There & Around

🚃 The Biscayne Trolley runs up Brickell Ave, then up Biscayne and zigzags over to 29th St and up to 39th St – handy for both districts. The Wynwood Trolley gets you closer; it goes from 15th St near the Adrienne Arsht Center up and over to NW 2nd Ave. Both are free.

Wynwood & the Design District Map on p92

Top Sight 📷
Wynwood Walls

The launch of the Wynwood Walls created waves in the contemporary-art world that ripple to this day. It came in the form of eye-popping, color-saturated murals blanketing the walls of a former warehouse district. Artists from around the world have added their touch to this ever-changing open-air gallery, transforming Wynwood into an epicenter for public art.

◎ MAP P92, C6

www.thewynwoodwalls.com

NW 2nd Ave, btwn 25th & 26th Sts

admission free

The Art

One of the most extraordinary features of the Wynwood Walls is that nothing here remains the same, which is perhaps an appropriate metaphor for the ephemeral nature of street art in general. The average lifespan for a mural here is less than one year before it's painted over by another artist – surprising, given the stunning quality of work on display.

Since the founding of the project, more than 50 artists from 16 different countries have painted on the walls. Among the first crop of talented artists was Shepard Fairey, whose 'Obey' street tags (depicting the mug of Andre the Giant) and 'Hope' posters (with Obama's portrait) helped garner him wide-reaching acclaim. Other famous artists who've installed their work include Os Gemeos (twin brothers who hail from Brazil), French painter Invader, the Japanese artist Aiko and the Portuguese Alexandre Farto (aka Vhils), who 'carves' rather than paints – at times even using a jack hammer to create realistic portraits on concrete walls.

Unlike in many gallery paintings, the street art contains a visceral edge that explores topics like homelessness, police brutality, disenfranchisement, rampant materialism and the ever-widening chasm of inequality between the haves and the have-nots. There are also fantastical science-fiction scenes, dynamic color swaths swirling with abstract patterns and beautiful portraits of positive people. The Dalai Lama, Aung San Suu Kyi, Martin Luther King Jr, Bob Marley and, uh, Yoda, have all graced the walls at one time or another.

The Wynwood Walls Shop

Is there a gift shop here? Of course there is. The on-site **Wynwood Walls Shop** (📞 305-576-8205; https://thewynwoodwalls.com/wynwood-walls-shop-2; 2520 NW 2nd Ave; 🕙 10:30am-7pm Sun-Thu,

★ Top Tips

○ Wynwood Walls offers private walking tours (from $20 per person) led by street artists. Book online.

○ You can learn more about the neighborhood's street art and its gallery scene on a walking tour offered by Wynwood Art Walk (p89).

○ A great time to see the neighborhood at its most celebratory is during the Wynwood Art Walk Block Party (p96), held on the second Saturday of the month.

✗ Take a Break

Grab some delicious Mexican-style street food at Coyo Taco (p97).

Stay caffeinated at Panther Coffee (p97), serving the best pour-overs in Miami.

Evolution of an Arts District

Wynwood was one of Miami's most prominent Puerto Rican neighborhoods in the latter portion of the 20th century, and proud of its nickname little San Juan. This all changed in the early 2000s, thanks in part to the efforts of real estate developer Tony Goldman.

Goldman was already credited with preserving much of South Beach via the purchase of some of that area's most iconic deco buildings. Outside of its residential blocks, Wynwood was the home of many empty warehouses and abandoned stores. Cheap rents combined with relative proximity to Downtown had already attracted artists. Goldman, long a patron of and advocate for street art began buying up properties with the intent of unleashing a master plan: he would invite artists from around the world to create the largest collection of street art ever assembled in Miami.

Goldman started with the warehouse complex of six buildings on 25th to 26th Sts. Using the buildings (perfectly configured as they lacked windows) as blank canvases, his roster of artists set to work. Art-world superstar Jeffrey Deitch helped co-curate the first year's project in 2009. Artists were offered free airfare, hotel accommodation and all the supplies they needed, then given free rein. The plan was a smash success. That year at Art Basel, thousands of visitors came to see the street murals and the Wynwood Walls were the talk of the town.

Then more gallery owners, restaurants and bars came; their success propelled by the early-21st-century trend of young suburbanites moving back into city centers. The gentrification of Wynwood was rapid, if not break neck. The Wynwood Art Walks helped cement the area as a go-to nightspot for residents who wanted the style and glitz of South Beach minus the enormous tourist crowds and the worst excesses of shallow commercialism. Today Wynwood has evolved far past hipster cliches to become a mainstream nexus of the Miami social scene.

to 9pm Fri & Sat) sells all kinds of gifts, toys, prints and other objects of interest related to the Wynwood Walls exhibits, or the artists behind the murals. Some say the presence of the shop chips away at what counterculture cred Wynwood Walls had built up; others point out that hey, this is Miami, and every institution has a side hustle.

Enjoying the Arts

The Wynwood Walls helped turn Wynwood into an arts district. A mix of bohemians and yuppies, innovators and influencers turned the neighborhood into Miami's most buzzed about slice of urban geography. Part of the appeal of this place is not just the art; it's an almost overwhelming wave of dining, nightlife and shopping that has sprouted up amid the art.

The explosion of murals outside of the Walls means Wynwood can lay claim to the largest concentration of street art in the world. In addition, dozens of art galleries are scattered throughout the neighborhood, with new spaces opening all the time. A nice way of seeing them and getting in some free wine and cheese is attending the famous **Wynwood Art Walks** (📞305-814-9290; www.wynwoodart walk.com; tours from $29).

The neighborhood covers a large area, with attractions spread across many blocks. However, you'll find the densest concentration of sights, murals and galleries along NW 2nd Ave and just off this street. A handy approach is to head north from 23rd St to about 29th St, dipping in and out of intersecting streets along the way.

The stomping grounds of 'Wypsters' (Wynwood hipsters; those who enjoy, staff and provide content for the neighborhood's galleries) shift month by month as guerrilla galleries, new murals, graffiti, cafes, restaurants and studio spaces spread across town. It's often difficult to recommend specific galleries since one great show might be followed by a dud, but here are a few favorites:

○ Margulies Collection at the Warehouse (p94)

○ De La Cruz Collection (p91)

○ Bakehouse Art Complex (p94)

○ Locust Projects (p91)

Walking Tour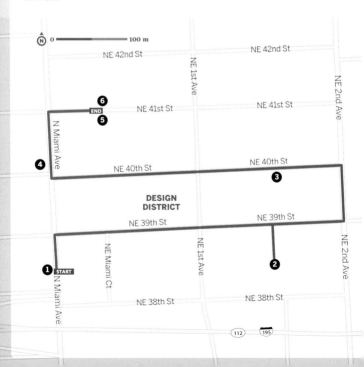

Art & High Design

One neighborhood that more than lives up to its name is the Design District, a compact area sprinkled with galleries, high-end designer boutiques and places to eat. You'll also find some lovely contemporary architecture throughout, along with intriguing outdoor installations that bring the art out of the gallery and into the public sphere. The main drags are along NW 39th and 40th Sts.

Walk Facts
Start Locust Projects
End De La Cruz Collection
Length 1 mile; two hours

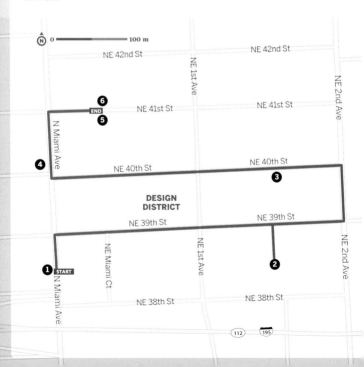

❶ Locust Projects

Locust Projects (☏305-576-8570; www.locustprojects.org; 3852 N Miami Ave; admission free; ⏱11am-5pm Tue-Sat) has become a major name for emerging artists in the contemporary gallery scene. Run by artists as a nonprofit collective since 1998, LP has exhibited work by more than 250 local, national and international artists over the years. The gallery often hosts site-specific installations by artists and is willing to take a few more risks than more commercial venues.

❷ Palm Court

At the epicenter of the design district is this pretty **courtyard** (140 NE 39th St), which opened just before Art Basel back in 2014. It's set with tall palm trees, two floors of high-end retailers and one eye-catching sculpture. The Fly's Eye Dome is a geodesic dome that appears to be floating (or gently submerged) in a square fountain.

❸ Michael's Genuine

This long-running upscale **tavern** (☏305-573-5550; www.michaels genuine.com; 130 NE 40th St; mains lunch $16-29, dinner $17-48; ⏱11:30am-11pm Mon-Sat, to 10pm Sun) combines excellent service with a well-executed menu of wood-fired dishes, bountiful salads and raw bar temptations (including oysters and stone crabs). Michael's tends to draw a well-dressed crowd and the place gets packed most days.

❹ Living Room

Reminding you that you're entering the Design District is a surreal public art installation of, yep, a living room – just the sort of thing you're supposed to shop for here. Actually this **Living Room** (cnr NW 40th St & N Miami Ave), by Argentine husband-and-wife team Roberto Behar and Rosario Marquardt, is an 'urban intervention' designed to criticize the disappearance of public space.

❺ Institute of Contemporary Art

For the last two decades the artistic output of this neighborhood has cleaved towards the bleeding edge of arts innovation, or at least the edge embraced by the contemporary art criticism scene. The **Institute of Contemporary Art** (☏305-901-5272; www.icamiami.org; 61 NE 41st St; admission free; ⏱11am-7pm Tue-Sun) is a great place to acquaint yourself with this aesthetic and the artists creating it.

❻ De La Cruz Collection

This 30,000-sq-ft **gallery** (☏305-576-6112; www.delacruzcollection.org; 23 NE 41st St; admission free; ⏱10am-4pm Tue-Sat) has a treasure trove of contemporary works scattered across three floors, which you can roam freely. Rosa and Carlos de la Cruz, who originally hail from Cuba, have particularly strong holdings in postwar German paintings, as well as fascinating works by Jim Hodges, Ana Mendieta and Félix González-Torres.

Wynwood & the Design District

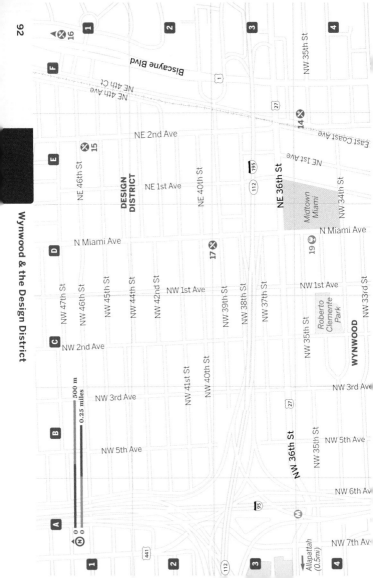

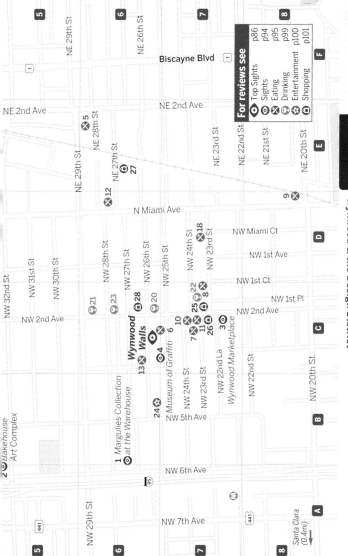

Wynwood & the Design District

NE 29th St
NE 26th St
Biscayne Blvd
NE 2nd Ave
NE 2nd Ave
NE 28th St
NE 27th St
NE 29th St
NE 23rd St
NE 22nd St
NE 21st St
NE 20th St

For reviews see
⊙ Top Sights p86
⊙ Sights p94
⊗ Eating p95
🍸 Drinking p99
✦ Entertainment p100
🛍 Shopping p101

N Miami Ave
NW Miami Ct
NW 1st Ave
NW 1st Ct
NW 1st Pl
NW 2nd Ave

NW 32nd St
NW 31st St
NW 30th St
NW 28th St
NW 27th St
NW 26th St
NW 25th St
NW 24th St
NW 23rd St

NW 2nd Ave

Wynwood Walls

Museum of Graffiti

1 Margulies Collection at the Warehouse

2 Bakehouse Art Complex

Wynwood Marketplace

NW 22nd La
NW 2nd Ave
NW 22nd Ave
NW 20th St

NW 5th Ave
NW 6th Ave
NW 7th Ave
NW 29th St

Santa Clara (0.4mi)

95

441

441

Sights

Margulies Collection at the Warehouse

GALLERY

1 ⊙ MAP P92, B6

Encompassing 45,000 sq ft, this vast not-for-profit exhibition space houses one of the best art collections in Wynwood – Martin Margulies' awe-inspiring 4000-piece collection includes sculptures by Isamu Noguchi, George Segal, Richard Serra and Olafur Eliasson, among many others, plus sound installations by Susan Philipsz and jaw-dropping room-sized works by Anselm Kiefer. Thought-provoking, large-format installations are the focus at the Warehouse, and you'll see works by some leading 21st-century artists here. (📞305-576-1051; www.margulieswarehouse.com; 591 NW 27th St; adult/student $10/5; ⏰11am-4pm Tue-Sat mid-Oct–Apr)

Bakehouse Art Complex

GALLERY

2 ⊙ MAP P92, A5

One of the pivotal art destinations in Wynwood, the Bakehouse has been an arts incubator since well before the creation of the Wynwood Walls. Today this former bakery houses galleries and some 60 studios, and the range of works is quite impressive. Check the schedule for upcoming artist talks and other events. (BAC; 📞305-576-2828; www.bacfl.org; 561 NW 32nd St; admission free; ⏰noon-5pm; 🅿)

Wynwood Marketplace

MARKET

3 ⊙ MAP P92, C7

An enormous open-air market-place takes over several blocks of Wynwood real estate on week-end evenings, and plays hosts to artisan shops, food trucks, a performance stage, live music, art exhibitions, etc. The Marketplace is more or less a weekly carnival, and given Miami's consistently good weather, it's a pleasant one to stroll. While booze is sold, the vibe is family friendly. (📞305-461-2700; www.wynwood-marketplace.com; 2250 NW 2nd Ave; ⏰1pm-2am Fri & Sat, noon-9pm Sun)

Museum of Graffiti

MUSEUM

4 ⊙ MAP P92, C7

The Museum of Graffiti gives visitors a quick dive into the history of this particular art form, which is so obviously and brilliantly in evidence on the urban blocks of surrounding Wynwood. It's a bit small, but passionate: there are kids' art classes on Sundays (11am, free with parent admission), photos from graffiti's earliest days, temporary exhibitions from graffiti masters, and beginners' graffiti workshops ($100, 2pm Sat). The gift shop alone is a must for anyone who likes graffiti or pop art. (📞786-580-4678; https://museumofgraffiti.com; 299 NW 25th St; adult/child $16/free; ⏰11am-7pm Wed-Mon; 👪)

Eating

Enriqueta's
LATIN AMERICAN **$**

5 ✕ MAP P92, E6

Enriqueta's is an outpost of pre-gentrification Miami in the heart of that city's most gentrified neighborhood, a roadhouse diner where local Spanish speakers, as opposed to international installation artists, rule the roost. Notable for its excellent coffee, *pan con bistec* (steak sandwiches), *croquetas* (croquettes), Cuban sandwiches, and daily specials such as *picadillo* (spiced ground beef) and *lechón asado* (roast pork). (📞305-573-4681; 186 NE 29th St; mains $6-14; ⏰6am-4pm Mon-Fri, to 2pm Sat)

Kyu
FUSION **$$**

6 ✕ MAP P92, C7

Kyu has been dazzling locals and food critics alike with its creative Asian-inspired dishes, most of which are cooked over the open flames of a wood-fired grill. Try the Florida red snapper, beef tenderloin and a magnificent head of cauliflower. There's also grilled octopus, soft-shell-crab steamed buns and smoked beef brisket. Book well ahead, or turn up and wait (usually around an hour).

The bar is the go-to spot for creative cocktails (with drink and food specials during happy hour). (📞786-577-0150; www.kyumiami.com; 251 NW 25th St; sharing plates $17-44; ⏰noon-11:30pm Mon-Sat, 11am-10:30pm Sun, bar to 1am Fri & Sat; 🍸)

Installation by Giz and Ghost, Museum of Graffiti

Monthly Art Fest

One of the best ways to take in the burgeoning Miami art scene is to join in the **Wynwood Art Walk Block Party** (☎305-461-2700; www.wynwoodartwalkblockparty.com; ☺1pm-midnight 2nd Sat of month), held on the second Saturday of every month. Many of the galleries around Wynwood host special events and art openings, with ever-flowing drinks (not always free), live music around the 'hood, food trucks and special markets.

Alter
MODERN AMERICAN $$$

7 ❌ MAP P92, C7

Alter's changing menu showcases high-quality Florida ingredients from sea and land in seasonally inspired dishes with Asian- and European-flavored haute cuisine. Expect dishes such as eggs with sea-scallop foam, truffle pearls and Siberian caviar, or 'Pelin' duck with dashi, turnip and Jamaican ginger beer. Reserve soon, preferably yesterday. (☎305-573-5996; www.altermiami.com; 223 NW 23rd St; set menu 5/7 courses $90/110; ☺7-11pm Tue-Sun)

1 800 Lucky
FOOD HALL $

8 ❌ MAP P92, C7

Another example of Wynwood becoming a sort of adult playground for cosmopolitan world wanderers, 1 800 Lucky tries to recreate an Asian food hall in the midst of South Florida. The atmosphere is excellent: red lanterns, booming lounge and hip-hop, a slick bar, beautiful people. The food is pretty good too, ranging from sashimi bowls to Thai-style chicken wings to Chinese pork belly buns.

The food hall more or less becomes an outdoor bar as the night wears on, as popular as the most packed Miami club. (☎305-768-9826; wwww.1800lucky.com; 143 NW 23rd St; mains $7-16; ☺noon-2am Mon-Thu, to 3am Fri-Sun)

Kush
AMERICAN $

9 ❌ MAP P92, D8

Gourmet burgers plus craft brews is the simple but winning formula at this lively eatery and drinking den on the southern fringe of Wynwood. Juicy burgers topped with hot pastrami, Florida avocados and other decadent options go down nicely with drafts from Sixpoint and Funky Buddha. There are great vegetarian options too, including a house-made black-bean burger and vegan jambalaya. (☎305-576-4500; www.kushwynwood.com; 2003 N Miami Ave; mains $12-16; ☺noon-11pm Sun-Tue, to midnight Wed & Thu, to 1am Fri & Sat; ❌)

Panther Coffee

CAFE $

10 ✖ MAP P92, C7

Miami's best independent coffee shop specializes in single-origin, small-batch roasts, fired up to perfection. Aside from sipping on a zesty brewed-to-order Chemex-made coffee (or a creamy latte), you can enjoy microbrews, wines and sweet treats. The front patio is a great spot for people-watching.

Panther also hosts cupping classes and occasional nights of live music, performance art and other events. There's also a **Sunset Harbour** (📞305-677-3952; 1875 Purdy Ave; coffees $3-6; ⏰7am-7pm) location in Miami Beach. (📞305-677-3952; www.panthercoffee. com; 2390 NW 2nd Ave; coffees $3-6; ⏰7am-9pm Sun-Thu, to 11pm Fri & Sat; 📶)

Coyo Taco

MEXICAN $

11 ✖ MAP P92, C7

If you're in Wynwood and craving tacos, this is the place to be. You'll have to contend with lines day or night, but those beautifully turned-out tacos are well worth the wait – and come in creative varieties such as chargrilled octopus, marinated mushrooms or crispy duck, along with the usual array of steak, grilled fish and roasted pork. (📞305-573-8228; www.coyo-taco. com; 2300 NW 2nd Ave; mains $7.50-13; ⏰11am-3am Mon-Sat, to 11pm Sun; 🍴)

SuViche

FUSION $

12 ✖ MAP P92, D6

SuViche is just fun: an open-sided setting of garrulous couples chatting over swinging chairs, graffiti-esque murals and good beats. The menu – and you may have guessed this based off the name – is a blend of Peruvian dishes (including half a dozen varieties of ceviche) and sushi, which goes down nicely with the creative *mac-erados* (pisco-infused cocktails).

Visit the website for other locations, including South Beach and Brickell. (📞305-501-5010; www. suviche.com; 2751 N Miami Ave; sushi $7-12, ceviche $8-15; ⏰11:30am-11pm Mon-Thu, to midnight Fri, noon-midnight Sat, noon-11pm Sun)

Zak the Baker

DELI $

13 ✖ MAP P92, C6

This kosher bakery is admired by all for its delicious breads, bagels and sandwiches. Lines will often stretch around the block for all of the above, but the wait is worth it. (📞786-294-0876; www.zakthebaker. com; 295 NW 26th St; sandwiches $8-17; ⏰7am-7pm Sun-Fri)

La Latina

LATIN AMERICAN $

14 ✖ MAP P92, E4

One of the best budget meals near the Design District can be found at La Latina, a Venezuelan diner that's popular with Midtown locals and artsy transplants to the area. Cheese and avocado *arepas* (corn cakes) are a treat for vegetarians, but there's a lot of meat, rice, beans and sweet plantains filling out the menu. (📞305-571-9655; www.lalatinamiami. com; 3509 NE 2nd Ave; mains $7-10; ⏰9am-10pm Sun-Thu, to 5am Fri & Sat; 🍴)

Buena Vista Deli
CAFE $

15 ❌ MAP P92, E1

Never mind the uninspiring name: French-owned Buena Vista Deli is a charming Parisian-style cafe that warrants a visit no matter the time of day. Come in the morning for fresh croissants and other bakery temptations, and later in the day for thick slices of quiche, big salads and hearty sandwiches – plus there's wine, beer and good coffee. On clear days, the sidewalk tables are the place to be. (📞305-576-3945; www.buenavistadeli.com; 4590 NE 2nd Ave; mains $8-15; ⏰7am-11pm)

Cake Thai
THAI $$

16 ❌ MAP P92

Chef Phuket Thongsodchaveondee (who goes by the name 'Cake') is a Godfather of Thai cuisine in Miami, whipping up roasted duck salad, Panang pork belly, baby back ribs with garlic and black pepper, and pad thai with prawns – plus several variations of fried rice for good measure. (📞786-534-7906; www. cakethaikitchen.com; 7919 Biscayne Blvd; mains $12-24; ⏰noon-9:30pm Mon-Thu, to 11pm Fri & Sat, to 10:30pm Sun; 🍴)

Salty Donut

Harry's Pizzeria

PIZZA $$

17 🍴 MAP P92, D3

A stripped-down yet sumptuous dining experience awaits pizza lovers in the Design District. Harry's tiny kitchen and dining room dishes out deceptively simple wood-fired pizzas topped with creative ingredients (shrimp, lemon and manchego, or spicy pepperoni). Add in some not-to-be missed appetizers like polenta fries and you have a great, haute-cuisine meal served for a very reasonable rate.

There are also non-pizza hits like a meatball sandwich and eggplant Parmesan, old school comfort food that's been considerably sexed up. (📞786-275-4963; www.harryspizzeria.com; 3918 N Miami Ave; pizzas $13-17, mains $12-24; ⏱11:30am-10pm Sun-Thu, to midnight Fri & Sat; 🚼)

Salty Donut

DOUGHNUTS $

18 🍴 MAP P92, D7

Although 'artisanal doughnuts' sounds pretentious, no one can deny the merits of these artfully designed creations featuring seasonal ingredients. Maple and bacon, guava and cheese, and brown butter and salt are a few classics, joined by changing hits such as pistachio and white chocolate or strawberry and lemon cream. (📞305-639-8501; www.saltydonut. com; 50 NW 23rd St; doughnuts $3-6; ⏱7:30am-6pm Tue-Fri, from 8am Sat & Sun; 🛜)

Drinking

The Sylvester

BAR

19 🍺 MAP P92, D4

The Sylvester wants to push the neighborhood bar vibe, with its vintage furniture, long, lounge-y layout and classic cocktails. But the neighborhood that surrounds the bar is Wynwood, a hotbed of contemporary art and bleeding-edge design, so this is still a spot where beautiful people pack in wall to wall and the music gets pumping, especially on weekends. (📞305-814-4548; www. thesylvesterbar.com; 3456 N Miami Ave; ⏱5pm-2am Tue-Thu & Sun, to 3am Fri & Sat)

Wood Tavern

BAR

20 🍺 MAP P92, C6

The crowd here is local kids who want something stylish, but don't want South Beach – Wood Tavern has both atmosphere and aesthetic. Food specials are cheap, the beer selection is excellent and the crowd is friendly. The outdoor space has picnic benches, a wooden stage complete with bleachers and a giant Jenga game, and an attached art gallery with rotating exhibits. (📞305-748-2828; www.facebook. com/woodtavern; 2531 NW 2nd Ave; ⏱5pm-3am Tue-Sat, 3pm-midnight Sun, 5pm-2am Mon)

Boxelder
BAR

21 🚇 MAP P92, C6

This long, narrow space is a beer-lover's Valhalla, with a curated menu of brews from near and far, though its 20 rotating beer taps leave pride of place for South Florida beers. There's also more than 100 different varieties by the bottle. What keeps the place humming is Boxelder's friendly, down-to-earth vibe.

Adam and Nicole, who run the place, really know their beers, and have gathered quite a following. Boxelder also hosts art openings, special beer nights (when local brewers release new batches) and other events. (📞305-942-7769; www.bxldr.com; 2817 NW 2nd Ave; ⏰4pm-midnight Mon, 1pm-midnight Tue-Thu, to 2am Fri & Sat, to 10pm Sun)

Gramps
BAR

22 🚇 MAP P92, C7

Friendly and unpretentious (just like some grandpas), Gramps always has something afoot whether it's live music and DJs, dueling synthesizers (awesome) or bingo. The big draw though is really just the sizable backyard that's perfect for alfresco drinking and socializing.

A little shop called **Pizza Tropical** serves slices ($4 to $6) out in the backyard. It was started by Frank Pinello, who used to host Vice TV's *The Pizza Show*, which is all to say: this is pretty good pie. (📞305-699-2669; www.gramps.com;

176 NW 24th St; ⏰11am-1am Sun-Wed, to 3am Thu-Sat)

R House
BAR

23 🚇 MAP P92, C6

R House specializes in a lot: cocktails, happy hours, and shareable happy hour bites ($3 to $7).But it's best known for its immensely popular drag brunch. You need to reserve seats ($45 to $65, food included) *way* in advance for this raucous affair, a nonstop performance by a super-talented drag cast that has a deserved reputation as one of the best midday parties in Miami. (📞305-576-0201; www.rhousewynwood.com; 2727 NW 2nd Ave; ⏰3-10pm Wed & Thu, to 3am Fri, 11:30am-3am Sat, to 9pm Sun, brunch 11:30am & 2:30pm Sat & Sun)

Entertainment

Light Box at Goldman Warehouse
PERFORMING ARTS

24 ⭐ MAP P92, B6

The Miami Light Project, a non-profit cultural foundation, stages a wide range of innovative theater, dance, music and film performances at this intimate theater. It's in Wynwood, and a great place to discover cutting-edge works by artists you might not have heard of. It is particularly supportive of troupes from South Florida. (📞305-576-4350; www.miamilight project.com; 404 NW 26th St)

Shopping

Nomad Tribe
CLOTHING

25 🔒 MAP P92, C7

This boutique earns high marks for carrying only ethically and sustainably produced merchandise. You'll find cleverly designed jewelry from Miami-based Kathe Cuervo, Osom brand socks (made of upcycled thread), ecologically produced graphic T-shirts from Thinking MU, and THX coffee and candles (which donates 100% of profits to nonprofit organizations), among much else. (📞305-364-5193; www.nomadtribeshop.com; 2301 NW 2nd Ave; ⏱noon-8pm)

Harold Golen Gallery
ART

26 🔒 MAP P92, C7

Original artwork is exhibited at this small gallery, mainly of a very animation/anime/tiki-influenced pop art variety, often painted in rainbow palettes set to neon levels of bright. There is also a ton of art-adjacent gifts – posters, books, stickers, patches and prints – influenced by this playful aesthetic. One of the few Wynwood galleries younger kids will get a kick out of.

(📞305-989-3359; https://haroldgolen.gallery; 2294 NW 2nd Ave; ⏱noon-7pm)

Art by God
GIFTS & SOUVENIRS

27 🔒 MAP P92, E6

Purses? Jackets? *Psssht*. When we go shopping, we like to buy fossilized dinosaur poop, and clumps of amethysts, and stuffed full-sized zebras. It's all on offer at Art by God, as well as rhino heads, dinosaur bones, and more portable things like home furnishings from all of earth's continents. (📞305-573-3011; www.artbygod.com; 60 NE 27th St; ⏱10am-5pm Mon-Fri, 11am-4pm Sat)

Malaquita
ARTS & CRAFTS

28 🔒 MAP P92, C6

This artfully designed store has merchandise you won't find elsewhere, including lovely handblown vases, embroidered clothing, Mesoamerican tapestries, vibrantly painted bowls, handwoven palm baskets and other fair-trade objects – some of which are made by indigenous artisans in Mexico. (www.malaquitadesign.com; 2613 NW 2nd Ave; ⏱11am-8pm)

Explore ⊚
Little Havana

The Cuban-ness of Little Havana is slightly exaggerated for visitors, though it's still an atmospheric area to explore, with the sound of salsa spilling into Calle Ocho (SW 8th St), the heart of the neighborhood. Keep an eye out for murals; older art often references the Cuban revolution, while newer pieces contain contemporary references to hip-hop and the Miami Heat basketball team.

The Short List

○ **Cubaocho (p111)** *Catching a live performance by top artists from Cuba and beyond at this intimate and atmospheric music and arts venue.*

○ **Máximo Gómez Park (p107)** *Watching rapid-fire domino games unfold in Little Havana's liveliest open-air gathering spot.*

○ **Little Havana Art District (p107)** *Visiting the latest Latin-themed art exhibitions at galleries dotting the area.*

○ **Tower Theater (p108)** *Catching an indie movie at this excellent theater, fronted by a classic deco facade.*

Getting There & Around

🚌 The number 8 bus from Brickell Station makes the 15-minute journey out to Little Havana every 10 to 20 minutes. Note that it travels westbound on 7th St and eastbound (back towards Downtown) on 8th St.

🚲 There is one handy Citi Bike station here, at SW 8th St and 10th Ave.

Little Havana Map on p106

DE
ASALTO

2506

17 DE Abril 1961

Top Sight

Cuban Memorial Boulevard Park

Miami is home to the largest Cuban diaspora in the world, a group that now dominates the social and political life of the city. This boulevard is a testament to the enormous cultural significance of an island that thousands of Miamians have never set foot on, yet that still remains, in a vital way, a place they consider integral to their identity.

◎ MAP P106, D3

SW 13th Ave, btwn 8th & 11th Sts

A Multitude of Monuments

Taken on its own, the Memorial Boulevard Park is a skinny public space occupying the median of SW 13th Ave, taking up four blocks of real estate. There are statues and memorials popping up every few feet, and it takes some cultural or historical context to appreciate many of them.

The Eternal Torch of Brigade 2506 (pictured) is dedicated to those soldiers who gave their lives in the 1961 Bay of Pigs Invasion of Cuba. The theme of anti-communism is also given a nod in a bronze statue of Nestor 'Tony' Izquierdo, a Bay of Pigs veteran who went on to fight for Nicaragua's right-wing Somoza regime.

Other monuments include a statue of the Virgin Mary; a bust of Antonio Maceo Grajales, a hero of the Cuban War of Independence; a bronze map of Cuba; and the *Plaza de Los Periodistas Cubanos*, dedicated to Cuban journalists critical of the Castro regime.

The Ceiba Tree

In the middle of the block connecting SW 10th St and Calle Ocho (SW 8th St) is a striking Ceiba tree, with spindly branches and a spidery root system. Ceiba trees feature heavily in the folklore of the Caribbean and Latin America, and this Ceiba is important to practitioners of *Santería*, an Afro-Cuban religion that blends traditional West African Yoruba beliefs with Roman Catholicism in a manner similar to (but distinct from) *vodun* (voodoo). You may also spot candles and the occasional offering of rum or tobacco.

★ Top Tips

o The park is effectively always open, but is best visited in the early morning or around sunset; the heat of the day is less baking and there is sometimes an air of quiet (for Miami) reverence.

o The park is a five-minute walk from Maximo Gomez Park, where Cuban men while away the hours with cigars and domino matches.

✕ Take a Break

Grab one of the freshest fruit smoothies of your life and enjoy the people watching at Los Pinareños Frutería (p108), a tropical fruit stand par excellence.

El Nuevo Siglo (p107) is a grocery store with a hot-food counter that serves wonderful Cuban cuisine, just a few steps from the Boulevard Park.

Little Havana

For reviews see

◉	Top Sights	p104
◎	Sights	p107
✖	Eating	p107
◐	Drinking	p108
✪	Entertainment	p109
⊕	Shopping	p111

◉ Cuban Memorial Boulevard Park

Cuban Memorial Blvd

Máximo Gómez Park

Tower ◉ Theater

LITTLE HAVANA

Little Havana Art District

CORAL WAY

SW 8th St (Calle Ocho)

SW 7th St

Sights

Máximo Gómez Park   PARK

1 ◎ MAP P106, C3

Little Havana's most evocative reminder of Cuba is Máximo Gómez Park ('Domino Park'), where the sound of elderly men trash-talking over games of dominoes is harmonized with the quick clack-clack of slapping tiles – though the tourists taking photos all the while does take away from the experience. The heavy cigar smell and a sunrise-bright mural of the 1994 Summit of the Americas add to the atmosphere. (cnr SW 8th St & SW 15th Ave; ⏱9am-6pm)

Little Havana Art District   AREA

2 ◎ MAP P106, C3

This particular stretch of Little Havana is the epicenter of the **Viernes Culturales** (Cultural Fridays; www.viernesculturales.org; ⏱7-11pm 3rd Fri of month) celebration and has a handful of galleries and studios still in business that are worth a browse. (Calle Ocho, btwn SW 15th & 17th Aves)

Eating

El Nuevo Siglo   LATIN AMERICAN $

3 ✖ MAP P106, D3

Clouds of locals come to El Nuevo Siglo supermarket and rock up at the shiny black counter for delicious cooking at excellent prices, plus unfussy ambience. Everything is good: nibble on roast meats, fried yucca, tangy Cuban sandwiches, grilled snapper with rice, beans and plantains, and other daily specials. (☏305-854-1916; 1305 SW 8th St; mains $7-13; ⏱7am-9pm)

Versailles   CUBAN $

4 ✖ MAP P106, A3

Versailles (ver-*sigh*-yay) is an institution – one of the mainstays of Miami's Cuban gastronomic scene, and perhaps the most iconic Cuban restaurant in the nation. Try the excellent black bean soup or the fried yucca before moving onto heartier meat and seafood plates. Generations of Cuban Americans, along with Miami's Latin political elite, all rub elbows here. (☏305-444-0240; www.versaillesrestaurant.com; 3555 SW 8th St; mains $6-21; ⏱8am-1am Mon-Thu, to 2:30am Fri & Sat, 9am-1am Sun)

Doce Provisions   MODERN AMERICAN $$

5 ✖ MAP P106, E2

For a break from old-school Latin eateries, stop in at Doce Provisions. The industrial interior is stylish and sets the stage for dining on creative American fare – rock shrimp mac 'n' cheese, fried chicken with sweet plantain waffle, short-rib burgers and truffle fries – plus local microbrews. Brunch is justifiably popular on Sunday (11am to 3pm). There's a nice leafy terrace out back. (☏786-452-0161; www.doceprovisions.com; 541 SW 12th Ave; mains $12-25; ⏱noon-3:30pm

Iconic Cinema

Although most people don't go to Little Havana to watch a movie, there's much to recommend the **Tower Theater** (Map p106, C3; 305-237-2463; www.towertheatermiami.com; 1508 SW 8th St; tickets $11.75). This elegant 1920s movie house has a fine deco facade and screens thought-provoking indie and avant-garde fare – with English films subtitled in Spanish. It's a major icon for the neighborhood.

& 5-10pm Mon-Thu, noon-3:30pm & 5-11pm Fri, noon-11pm Sat, noon-9pm Sun)

Taqueria Viva Mexico   MEXICAN $

6 🍴 MAP P106, E2

Head up busy 12th Ave for some of the best tacos in Little Havana. From a takeout window, smiling Latin ladies dole out heavenly tacos topped with steak, tripe, sausage and other meats. You can also grab a quesadilla ($6 to $12), if that's your thing. There are a few outdoor tables – or get it to go.

On the downside, there's nothing here for vegetarians. (786-350-6360; 502 SW 12th Ave; tacos $2.50-3; 🕙11am-9pm Tue-Thu, to 11pm Fri & Sat, to 6pm Sun)

San Pocho   COLOMBIAN $

7 🍴 MAP P106, F3

For a quick journey to Colombia, head to friendly, always hopping San Pocho. The meat-centric menu features hearty platters such as *bandeja paisa* (with grilled steak, rice, beans, fried plantains, an egg, an *arepa* and fried pork skin). There's also *mondongo*

(tripe soup) as well as Colombian-style tamales and requisite sides such as *arepas* (corn cakes). (305-854-5954; www.sanpocho. com; 901 SW 8th St; mains $6.50-17; 🕙7am-8pm Mon-Thu, to 9pm Fri-Sun)

Azucar   ICE CREAM $

8 🍴 MAP P106, C3

One of Little Havana's oldest ice-cream parlors serves delicious ice cream just like *abuela* (grand-mother) used to make. Deciding isn't easy with dozens of tempting flavors, including rum raisin, dulce de leche, guava, mango, cinnamon, jackfruit and lemon basil. (305-381-0369; www.azucaricecream. com; 1503 SW 8th St; ice cream $4-6; 🕙11am-9pm Mon-Wed, to 11pm Thu-Sat, to 10pm Sun)

Drinking

Los Pinareños Frutería   JUICE BAR

9 🍹 MAP P106, D3

Nothing says refreshment on a sultry Miami afternoon like a cool glass of fresh juice (or *batidos* – milkshakes) at this fruit and veggie stand, beloved by generations of Miamians. Sip a *guarapa* (sugar-cane extract) *batido* while roosters cluck and folks gossip and argue in Cuban-accented Spanish; this is as Miami as it gets, short of being in a Pitbull song. (☎ 305-285-1135; 1334 SW 8th St; snacks & drinks $3-6; ⏰ 7am-6pm Mon-Sat, to 3pm Sun)

Ball & Chain   BAR

10 🚇 MAP P106, C3

The Ball & Chain has survived several incarnations over the years. Back in 1935, when 8th St was more Jewish than Latino, it was the sort of jazz joint Billie Holiday would croon in. That iteration closed in 1957, but today's Ball & Chain is still dedicated to music and good times – specifically, Latin music and tropical cocktails.

There's always something on, whether it's ladies night, live salsa shows, and top-notch performers on weekends. (☎ 305-643-7820; www.ballandchainmiami.com; 1513 SW 8th St; ⏰ 11am-midnight Mon-Wed, to 2am Thu, to 3am Fri & Sat, to 1am Sun)

Entertainment

Cafe La Trova   LIVE MUSIC

11 ⭐ MAP P106, F3

A lot of Miami places try to (re) create a romanticized old Cuba. La Trova, with its wood accents, immaculately dressed bartenders, and faded Havana-esque walls, really executes the concept. Regular live shows featuring classic Cuban dance music accompanied by a crowd decked out in their best dresses and *guayaberas* (Cuban

Tower Theater

Northern Capital
of the Latin World

Miami may technically be part of the USA, but it's widely touted as the 'capital of the Americas' and the 'center of the New World.' That's a coup when it comes to marketing Miami to the rest of the world, and especially to the USA, where Latinos are now the largest minority. For the visitor, Miami seems salsa-fueled and packed with Latin American culture, which manifests in distinct shops, restaurants, street festivals and nightlife.

A Latin Migration

Miami's pan-Latin mix makes it incredibly ethnically diverse. At the turn of the 21st century, the western suburbs of Hialeah Gardens and Hialeah were numbers one and two respectively on the list of US areas where Spanish is spoken as a first language (over 90% of the population).

How did this happen? Many of Miami's Latinos arrived in this geographically convenient city as political refugees – Cubans fleeing Castro from around the 1960s, Venezuelans fleeing President Hugo Chávez (or his predecessors), Brazilians and Argentines running from economic woes, Mexicans and Guatemalans arriving to find work.

Latin American Business in Miami

The local economy has been boosted by the growth of Latin American businesses. Miami is the US headquarters of many Latin companies, including Televisa, a Mexican TV conglomerate. Miami is also home to Telemundo, one of the biggest Spanish-language broadcasters in the US, as well as MTV Networks Latin America and the Latin branch of the Universal Music Group.

Cuban Americans & Politics

Cubans have a strong influence on local and international politics in Miami. Conservative exile groups have often been characterized as extreme, many refusing to visit Cuba while the Castro family remained in power. Since the death of Fidel in 2016, however, exiles have leaned toward more engagement with Cuba. While there is still plenty of resentment among older Cubans, the newer generation – sometimes referred to as the 'YUCAs' (Young Urban Cuban Americans) – are more diverse in their opinions. With that said, even a Cuban American with committed left-wing politics may well have grown up with family members viciously persecuted by the Castro regime. Politics in Miami are far more nuanced than the city gets credit for.

dress shirts) is insanely fun; if the scene here doesn't get you dancing, we're not sure what will. (786-615-4379; www.cafelatrova. com; 971 SW 8th St; noon-midnight Mon-Thu, to 2am Fri & Sat, 11am-midnight Sun)

Cubaocho
LIVE PERFORMANCE

12 ⭐ MAP P106, C3

Jewel of the Little Havana Art District, Cubaocho is renowned for its concerts, with excellent bands from across the Spanish-speaking world. It's also a community center, art gallery and research outpost for all things Cuban. The interior resembles an old Havana cigar bar, yet the walls are decked out in artwork that references both the classical past of Cuban art and its avant-garde future. (305-285-5880; www.cubaocho.com; 1465 SW 8th St; 11am-3am)

Shopping

Havana Collection
CLOTHING

13 🔒 MAP P106, D3

One of the best and most striking collections of the classic traditional *guayaberas* in Miami can be found in this shop. Prices are high (plan on spending about $85 for a shirt), but so is the quality, so you can be assured of a long-lasting

product. (786-717-7474; www.facebook.com/TheHavanaCollection; 1421 SW 8th St; 10am-6pm)

La Isla
ART

14 🔒 MAP P106, C3

This hip outpost of the new(er) Little Havana showcases Cuban-inspired pop art, graphic design and clever gifts (a poster of a certain *Star Wars* droid smoking a cigar titled 'Arturito' had us cracking up). La Isla promotes a Cuba more rooted in contemporary cool than black-and-white photos of cigar rollers, and is a great spot for a unique souvenir. (786-317-3051; https://laislausa.com; 1561 SW 8th St; 9am-5pm)

Little Havana Visitors Center
GIFTS & SOUVENIRS

15 🔒 MAP P106, C3

This is more gift shop than actual information kiosk. You'll find riotously colorful Hawaiian-style button-down shirts, Panama hats and plenty of kitschy memorabilia (fridge magnets, coffee cups, Cuban-flag bottle openers, and so on). It also often offers a taste of Cuban coffee. (305-643-0017; www.facebook.com/lhvcmiami; 1600 SW 8th St; 10am-6pm Mon-Sat, to 3pm Sun)

Walking Tour 🥾

Key Biscayne Escape

Key Biscayne and neighboring Virginia Key are a quick and easy getaway from Downtown Miami. But once you've passed across those scenic causeways, you'll feel like you've been transported to a far-off tropical realm, with magnificent beaches, lush nature trails in state parks and aquatic adventures aplenty.

Getting There

🚌 Number 102 provides service from Brickell (near Brickell Station on SW 1st Ave) over the Rickenbacker Causeway and all the way down to the Bill Baggs Cape Florida State Park.

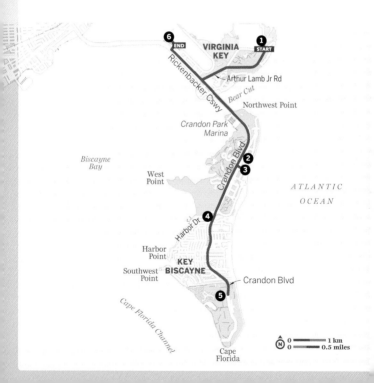

❶ Virginia Key Beach North Point Park

This attractive **green space** (off 3861 Rickenbacker Causeway, Virginia Key; per car weekday/weekend $6/8; ⊙8:15am-5pm Nov-Mar, 9:15am-6pm Apr-Oct) has several small, pleasing beaches and some short nature trails. Pretty waterfront views aside, the big reason for coming is to hire kayaks or paddleboards at Virginia Key Outdoor Center (www. vkoc.net).

❷ Marjory Stoneman Douglas Biscayne Nature Center

This child-friendly **nature center** (☏305-361-6767; www.biscayne naturecenter.org; 6767 Crandon Blvd, Crandon Park; admission free; ⊙10am-4pm; P 👫) is a great intro-duction to South Florida's unique ecosystems, with hands-on exhib-its as well as small aquariums full of local marine life. You can also stroll a nature trail through coastal hammock (hardwood forest) or enjoy the beach in front.

❸ Crandon Park

Crandon Park Beach stretches for 2 miles inside this 1200-acre **park** (☏305-365-2320; www.miamidade. gov/parks/crandon.asp; 6747 Crandon Blvd; per car weekday/weekend $5/7; ⊙sunrise-sunset; P 👫 👶). It's clean, not cluttered with tourists, and faces a lovely sweep of teal water. Much of the rest of the park consists of a dense coastal ham-mock and mangrove swamps.

❹ Golden Hog Gourmet

This **grocery store** (☏305-361-1300; https://thegoldenhogmarket. com; 91 Harbor Dr; mains $8-15; ⊙8am-9pm Mon-Sat, to 7pm Sun) might bill itself as 'gourmet', but you get a real mix of Key Biscayne characters here, from fishermen to well-off exiles from the mainland. It sells excellent cheese, bread, produce and sandwiches – perfect picnic fare.

❺ Bill Baggs Cape Florida State Park

If you don't make it to the Florida Keys, come to this **park** (☏786-582-2673; www.floridastateparks.org/ capeflorida; 1200 S Crandon Blvd; per car/person $8/2; ⊙8am-sunset, light-house 9am-5pm; P 👫 👶) for a taste of its unique island ecosystems. Explore a tangled clot of tropi-cal fauna and dark mangroves, interconnected by sandy trails and wooden boardwalks.

❻ Rusty Pelican

A panoramic skyline view draws the romantic to the **Rusty Peli-can** (☏305-361-0080; www.therusty pelican.com; 3201 Rickenbacker Causeway, Virginia Key; mains lunch $13-18, dinner $29-44; ⊙9am-8:30pm Sun-Wed, to 10pm Thu-Sat). But if you come for a sunset drink, the fresh air could certainly seduce you into staying for some of the surf 'n' turf menu.

Explore ◉

Coconut Grove

Coconut Grove was once a hippie colony, but these days its demographic is upper-middle-class, mall-going Miamians and college students. It's a pleasant place to explore, with intriguing shops and cafes, and a walkable village-like vibe. It's particularly appealing in the evenings, when residents fill the outdoor tables of its bars and restaurants. Coconut Grove backs onto the waterfront, with a pretty marina and some pleasant green spaces.

The Short List

∘ **Vizcaya Museum & Gardens (p116)** *Marveling at the astonishing collection of art and antiquities of this sprawling mansion.*

∘ **Kampong (p121)** *Wandering through verdant gardens in this green oasis.*

∘ **Barnacle Historic State Park (p119)** *Catching an evening concert on the grass at this early mansion.*

∘ **Ermita de la Caridad (p121)** *Visiting this architecturally striking church, while enjoying the bay views behind it.*

Getting There & Around

🚌 No 22 heads down SW 22nd Ave, then takes Tigertail Ave through the Grove and heads north up SW 27th Ave to the Coconut Grove Metrorail Station.

🚲 There are several Citi Bike kiosks in Coconut Grove, meaning you could cycle here from other parts of the city, particularly Downtown, which is about 5 miles away.

Coconut Grove Map on p120

Kampong (p121) IMAGEMD/SHUTTERSTOCK ©

Top Sight 📷
Vizcaya Museum & Gardens

They call Miami the Magic City and, if it is, this Italian villa, the housing equivalent of a Fabergé egg, is its most fairy-tale-like residence. Perched over the water, Vizcaya is a fascinating place to wander, with art-filled rooms, lavish antique furniture and picturesque gardens.

◉ MAP P120, E1

www.vizcaya.org

3251 S Miami Ave

adult/6-12yr/student & senior $22/10/15

🕤 9.30am-4.30pm Thu-Mon

Background

In 1912, the millionaire industrialist James Deering purchased 130 acres on the edge of Biscayne Bay and began making plans for his grand mansion. The project would take a decade of labor, performed by more than 1000 workers. Deering invested heavily in sculptures, paintings and furnishings from Europe, but also commissioned local artists for their work.

The House

The Renaissance-inspired mansion is a classic of Miami's Mediterranean Revival style. Thirty-four of its original 70 rooms are packed with exquisite artwork and beautifully made furnishings, some of which date back to the 15th century. The largest room is the informal living room, sometimes dubbed 'the Renaissance Hall' for its works dating from the 14th to the 17th centuries. The Admiral Carpet here was created for the grandfather of King Ferdinand of Spain in the 1400s.

The music room is intriguing for its beautiful wall canvases, which come from Northern Italy. It also has a harp, said to be made by the same artisan who crafted instruments for Marie Antoinette of France. The banquet hall, bedecked with tapestries that belonged to 19th-century English poets Robert and Elizabeth Barrett Browning. evokes the grandeur of Europe's imperial dining rooms.

The Gardens

Modeled on formal Italian gardens of the 17th and 18th centuries, these manicured spaces form a counterpoint to the wild mangroves beyond. The gardens were designed as a series of rooms, each with a unique sense of space and imbued with a different feeling. For inspiration, landscape architect Diego Suarez looked to the flora of South Florida as well as North Africa and Asia.

★ Top Tips

○ Once a month Vizcaya hosts 'Gardens by Moonlight' (adult/child $20/10), featuring live music, guided tours through the gardens and a performance by a different artist. It usually happens on a weekday near the full moon.

○ Go early in the day or in the afternoon to capture the best light for taking pictures.

○ For more insight into Vizcaya, hire the 90-minute audiotour ($5), which covers the history of the house, the gardens and James Deering. It's available in five different languages.

✕ Take a Break

The **Vizcaya Cafe** has made-to-order fare, including salads, empanadas, *mahi-mahi* (dorado fish) sandwiches and veggie (or meat) burgers.

Walking Tour

Wandering the Grove

Tree-lined streets, outdoor cafes and pretty waterfront green spaces give Coconut Grove a village-like vibe. Its compact center is more walkable than many other parts of Miami, which is a big draw for many residents. Grove folk would agree: strolling among its one-of-a-kind boutiques and neighborhood watering holes is one of the best ways to spend a sunny afternoon.

Walk Facts

Start Peacock Park

End Barnacle Historic State Park

Length 1 mile; three hours

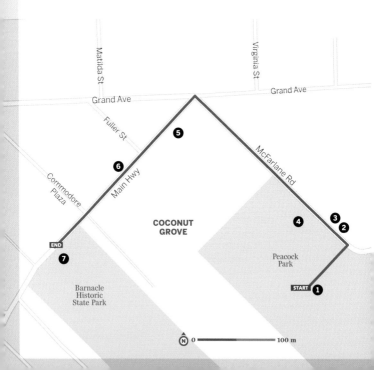

❶ Peacock Park

Along the waterfront, **Peacock Park** (2820 McFarlane Rd) serves as the great open backyard of Coconut Grove. Families stop by the playground, visitors join the action on the ball fields, while power walkers take in the view on a scenic stroll along the bayfront.

❷ Eva Munroe's Grave

It's a blink-and-you'll-miss-it situation, but in a small gated area by the library, you'll find the oldest marked grave in the city of Miami: that of Ms Eva Munroe (see also p122), who moved here from New York to cure the tuberculosis that still took her life in 1882.

❸ Coconut Grove Library

The Coconut Grove branch (p121) of the Miami-Dade Public Library System is encased in limestone walls, shaded by palm trees, and sits right in the direction of salt breezes blowing in off the bay. It's a very pretty place to browse books on South Florida.

❹ Glass & Vine

On the edge of Peacock Park, the star attraction of this **restaurant** (p123) is its outdoor setting. Offerings at lunch include tabbouleh and shrimp sandwiches; for dinner, try the charred cauliflower and sea scallops.

❺ Panther Coffee

Miami's best **coffee purveyor** (☎305-677-3952; www.panther coffee.com; 3407 Main Hwy; coffee $3-6; ⊙7am-7pm) has a branch in Coconut Grove, which serves boldly flavored pick-me-ups, plus heavenly bakery items. It's a great spot to linger over the paper or simply take in a slice of life in the Grove.

❻ Celestial Treasures

Your one-stop shop for spiritual and metaphysical needs, **Celestial Treasures** (☎305-461-2341; www. celestial-treasures.com; 3444 Main Hwy; ⊙11am-8pm Mon-Thu, to 10pm Fri & Sat, 10am-8pm Sun) has books, cards and more on Zen, Buddhism, Hinduism, Wicca, kabbalah and yoga. It also has staff psychics on hand.

❼ Barnacle Historic State Park

The 1891-built, five-acre pioneer residence of Ralph Monroe, Miami's first honorable snowbird, is open for guided tours, as is the surrounding **park** (☎305-442-6866; www.floridastateparks.org/thebarnacle; 3485 Main Hwy; admission $2, house tours adult/child $3/1; ⊙9am-5pm Wed-Mon; ⊞), which is a shady oasis for strolling. Barnacle hosts moonlight concerts and yoga, too.

Coconut Grove

Vizcaya Museum & Gardens

Biscayne Bay

Dinner Key Marina

Charthouse Dr

Pan American Dr

S Bayshore Dr

Darwin St

S Miami Ave

Tiger Tail Ave

SW 27th Ave

Chart house Dr

×15 4

×7

For reviews see	
◉ Top Sights	p116
◎ Sights	p121
✕ Eating	p122
🍷 Drinking	p125
🛍 Shopping	p125

Mary St

Rice St

Florida Ave

Grand Ave

Coconut Grove Library

McFarlane Rd

Eva Munroe's Grave

Peacock Park

Day Ave

Virginia St

Oak Ave

COCONUT GROVE

Orange St

Matilda St

Fuller St

Gifford La

Kirk Munroe Park

Florida Ave

Commodore Plaza

Barnacle Historic State Park

Via Abitare Way

Munroe Dr

SW 32nd Ave

Day Ave

Percival Ave

Margaret St

Oak Ave

Grand Ave

Thomas Ave

William Ave

Charles Ave

Franklin Ave

Main Hwy

Royal Rd

Elizabeth St

Frow Ave

Florida Ave

Plymouth Congregational Church

×11 6
14
8 12
10 18 13
16
17
9 ◎2 ◎5
◉1
3◎

400 m
0.2 miles

Sights

Kampong GARDENS

1 ◉ MAP P120, A4

David Fairchild, the Indiana Jones of the botanical world and founder of Fairchild Tropical Garden, would rest at the Kampong (Malay/Indonesian for 'village') in between journeys in search of beautiful and profitable plant life. Today this lush garden is listed on the National Register of Historic Places and the lovely grounds serve as a classroom for the National Tropical Botanical Garden. Self-guided tours (allow at least an hour) are available by appointment, as are $25 one-hour guided tours. (📞305-442-7169; https://ntbg.org/gardens/kampong; 4013 Douglas Rd; adult/child/senior & student $20/5/15; 🕙tours by appointment only 9:30am-3pm Tue-Fri, from 10:15am Sat)

Coconut Grove Library HISTORIC BUILDING

2 ◉ MAP P120, C3

Completed in 1963, the library has a photogenic design with oolitic limestone walls and a steep roof that pays homage to the original 1901 library that stood here. Inside, there's a small but well-curated reference section on South Florida. (📞305-442-8695; 2875 McFarlane Rd; 🕙9:30am-6pm Mon, Wed, Thu, to 5pm Sat, 11:30am-8pm Tue, closed Fri & Sun)

Plymouth Congregational Church CHURCH

3 ◉ MAP P120, A4

This 1917 coral church is striking, from its solid masonry to a hand-carved door from a Pyrenees monastery, which looks like it should be kicked in by Antonio Banderas carrying a guitar case full of explosives and Salma Hayek on his arm. Architecturally this is one of the finest Spanish Mission–style churches in a city that does not lack for examples of the genre. The church opens rarely, though all are welcome at the organ- and choir-led 10am Sunday service. (📞305-444-6521; www.plymouthmiami.org; 3400 Devon Rd; 🕙services 10am Sun; P)

Ermita de la Caridad MONUMENT

4 ◉ MAP P120, F1

The Catholic diocese purchased some of the bayfront land from

Biking the Grove

If you don't have a car, Citi Bike can be a fine way to visit Vizcaya (p116). Just ride along the water side of Bayshore Dr (you'll have to use the sidewalk in parts). Along the way, you can peak at marinas, leafy waterfront parks and detour to the Ermita de la Caridad (see above).

Coconut Grove Arts Festival

Coconut Grove retains a whiff of the bohemian even as it has become a considerably upper-middle-class enclave. The **Coconut Grove Arts Festival** (www.cgaf.com), held on Presidents' Day Weekend (before the third Monday in February) along Grand Ave, celebrates local artists, food and music, and is one of the most family-friendly arts events in Greater Miami.

Deering's Villa Vizcaya estate and built a shrine here for its displaced Cuban parishioners. Symbolizing a beacon, it faces the homeland, exactly 290 miles due south. There is also a mural that depicts Cuban history. Just outside the church is a grassy stretch of waterfront that makes a fine spot for a picnic. (☏305-854-2404; https://ermita.org; 3609 S Miami Ave; ⏱7am-5.30pm; mass noon Mon-Sat, 11am & 3pm Sun)

Eva Munroe's Grave   HISTORIC SITE

5 ◉ MAP P120, C3

Tucked into a small gated area near the Coconut Grove Library, you'll find the humble headstone of one Ms Eva Amelia Hewitt Munroe. Eva, who was born in New Jersey in 1856 and died in Miami in 1882, lies in the oldest American grave in Miami-Dade County (a sad addendum: local African American settlers died before Eva, but their deaths were never officially recorded). Eva's husband Ralph entered a deep depression, which he tried to alleviate by building the Barnacle, now one of the oldest historic homes in the area. (2875 McFarlane Rd)

Eating

Spillover   MODERN AMERICAN $$

6 ✗ MAP P120, C2

Tucked down a pedestrian strip near the CocoWalk, the Spillover serves locally sourced seafood and creative bistro fare in an affected vintage setting (cast-iron stools and recycled doors around the bar, suspenders-wearing staff, brassy jazz playing overhead). Come for crab cakes, buffalo shrimp tacos, spear-caught fish and chips, or a melt-in-your-mouth lobster Reuben.

On fine days, grab one of the outdoor tables, nicely set amid palm trees and a gurgling fountain. (☏305-456-5723; www.spillover miami.com; 2911 Grand Ave; mains $17-32; ⏱noon-10pm Sun-Thu, to 11pm Fri, 11am-11pm Sat, 11am-10pm Sun;)

Coral Bagels   DELI $

7 ✗ MAP P120, D1

Miami has a large 'Juban' (Jewish-Cuban) population, and this spot is sort of like a Juban given brick-and-mortar restaurant form. The buzzing little deli serves proper bagels, rich omelets and decadent potato pancakes with apple sauce and sour cream. You'll be hard-pressed to spend double digits, and you'll leave satisfied. (📞305-854-0336; www.coralbagels.com; 2750 SW 26th Ave; mains $7-11; ⏰6:30am-8pm Tue-Fri, 7am-8pm Sat, to 4pm Sun, 6:30am-3pm Mon; 🅿🍴)

Last Carrot VEGETARIAN $

8 🍴 MAP P120, B2

Going strong since the 1970s, and set in a decidedly unglamorous corner of Coconut Grove, the Last Carrot serves fresh juices, delicious pita sandwiches, avocado melts, veggie burgers and rather-famous spinach pies. The Carrot's endurance is testament to the quality of its good-for-your-body food served in a good-for-your-soul setting. (📞305-445-0805; 3133 Grand Ave; mains $5-9; ⏰10:30am-6pm Mon-Sat, 11am-4:30pm Sun; 🍴🚻)

Glass & Vine MODERN AMERICAN $$

9 🍴 MAP P120, C3

It's hard to beat the open-air setting of this wine-loving eatery on the edge of Peacock Park. Stop by for tabbouleh and shrimp sandwiches at lunch, or charred cauliflower and sea scallops at dinner. All of which go nicely with the extensive wine and cocktail menu. Excellent weekend brunches too. (📞305-200-5268; www.glassand vine.com; 2820 McFarlane Rd; mains $18-38; ⏰11:30am-3:30pm & 4-10pm Sun-Thu, to 11pm Fri & Sat)

Stone-crab claws, Monty's Raw Bar (p125)

LoKal

AMERICAN $$

10 ⊗ MAP P120, B2

This Coconut Grove joint does two things very well: burgers and craft beer. The former come in several variations, all utilizing excellent beef (bar the oat and brown-rice version). When in doubt, go for the frita, which adds in guava sauce, plus melted gruyere and crispy bacon. Wash it down with a Funky Buddha Hefeweizen or one of the 11 other craft brews on tap. (🖉305-442-3377; www.lokalmiami. com; 3190 Commodore Plaza; burgers $15-16; ⊙noon-10pm Mon & Tue, to 11pm Wed-Fri, 11:30am-11pm Sat, 11:30am-10pm Sun; ❄🖉👫)

Bombay Darbar

INDIAN $$

11 ⊗ MAP P120, C2

Indian food can be tough to find in Miami and all the more so in Coconut Grove, which makes Bombay Darbar even more of a culinary gem. Run by a couple from Mumbai, this upscale but friendly place hits all the right notes, with its beautifully executed tandooris and tikkas, best accompanied by piping-hot naan and flavor-bursting samosas. (🖉305-444-7272; www. bombaydarbar.com; 2901 Florida Ave; mains $17-22; ⊙noon-3pm Mon-Sat, 6-10pm Mon-Thu, to 11pm Fri & Sat, noon-10pm Sun; 🖉)

Lulu

MODERN AMERICAN $$

12 ⊗ MAP P120, B3

Lulu is the Grove's exemplar of using local, organic ingredients in its carefully prepared bistro dishes, all of which are best enjoyed at the outdoor tables. You can make a meal of tasty appetizers like roasted dates, Tuscan hummus or ahi tuna tartare, or go for more filling plates of slow-braised pork tacos and seared diver scallops. (🖉305-447-5858; https://luluinthe grove.com; 3105 Commodore Plaza; mains lunch $12-19, dinner $15-31; ⊙11:30am-10pm Sun-Thu, to 11pm Fri & Sat; 🖉)

GreenStreet Cafe

AMERICAN $$

13 ⊗ MAP P120, B3

Sidewalk spots don't get more popular than GreenStreet, where the Grove's pretty and gregarious congregate at sunset. The menu of high-end pub fare ranges from roast vegetable and goat cheese lasagna and mesclun endive salad to blackened *mahi-mahi* (dorado fish) and braised short ribs with polenta. (🖉305-444-0244; www. greenstreetcafe.net; 3468 Main Hwy; mains $15-31; ⊙7:30am-12:30am Sun-Tue, to 2am Wed-Sat)

Jaguar

LATIN AMERICAN $$

14 ⊗ MAP P120, C2

The menu at Jaguar spans the Latin world but the restaurant is particularly well known for its tasty and complex ceviche, which comes in over a half dozen varieties. Other mains include simple grilled fish and meats like Argentine-style beef tenderloin. (🖉305-444-0216; www.jaguarhg. com; 3067 Grand Ave; mains $16-28;

⏱11:30am-10pm Mon-Thu, to 11pm Fri, 11am-11pm Sat, 11am-10pm Sun)

Monty's Raw Bar
SEAFOOD $$

15 ✖ MAP P120, F1

Perched over the water, this breezy laid-back spot on Dinner Key has excellent seafood and beautiful bay views. Although Monty's is famous for stone-crab claws, there's plenty more on offer from fried cracked conch to barbecue ribs. Come at happy hour (4pm to 8pm) for $1 oysters and drink specials. (☎305-856-3992; www.montysrawbar.com; 2550 S Bayshore Dr; mains $13-25; ⏱11:30am-11:30pm Sun-Thu, to midnight Fri & Sat)

Drinking

Taurus
BAR

16 🍺 MAP P120, B3

The oldest bar in Coconut Grove is a cool mix of wood paneling, smoky-leather chairs, about 100 beers to choose from and a convivial vibe – as neighborhood bars go in Miami, this is one of the best. (☎305-529-6523; https://taurusbeerandwhiskey.com; 3540 Main Hwy; ⏱4pm-3am Mon-Fri, from noon Sat & Sun)

Shopping

Polished Coconut
FASHION & ACCESSORIES

17 🔒 MAP P120, A3

Colorful textiles from Central and South America are transformed into lovely accessories and home decor at this eye-catching store in the heart of Coconut Grove. You'll find handbags, satchels, belts, sun hats, pillows, bedspreads and table runners made by artisans inspired by traditional indigenous designs. (☎305-443-3220; www.facebook.com/PolishedCoconut; 3600 Grand Ave Village West; ⏱11am-6pm Mon-Sat, noon-5pm Sun)

Midori Gallery
ANTIQUES

18 🔒 MAP P120, B3

Filled with antiques and oddities from across Asia, the Midori Gallery also surprises: here a lacquer Japanese sake flash, there a standing Burmese Buddha, around the corner a neolithic vase from China. This feels like the sort of shop Indiana Jones uses to decorate his study. (☎305-443-3399; www.midorigallery.com; 3168 Commodore Plaza; ⏱11am-6pm Tue-Sat)

Explore
Coral Gables

The lovely city of Coral Gables, filled with a pastel rainbow of Mediterranean-style buildings, feels a world removed from the rest of Miami. Here you'll find pretty banyan-lined streets and a walkable village-like center, dotted with shops, cafes and restaurants. The big draws are the striking Biltmore Hotel, a lush tropical garden and one of America's loveliest swimming pools.

The Short List

○ Biltmore Hotel (p130) *Exploring the opulent corridors and grand courtyards inside Miami's most decadent hotel from the Jazz Age.*

○ Fairchild Tropical Garden (p128) *Walking amid flittering butterflies, past bubbling brooks and flowering species from the rainforest.*

○ Venetian Pool (p134) *Splashing about the faux grottoes and coral cliffs of this whimsical masterpiece.*

○ Coral Gables Museum (p136) *Learning about the curious history of this planned community-city inside a photogenic deco building.*

○ Matheson Hammock Park (p135) *Getting a dose of nature and taking a dip in a tidal pool at this leafy, mangrove-fringed park.*

Getting There & Around

🚌 The free Coral Way trolley travels from Downtown Miami to the heart of Coral Gables at Ponce de Leon Blvd and Coral Way (SW 22nd St).

🚗 It's a fairly straightforward drive, with one approach via SW 3rd Ave and on to SW 22nd St. There's ample (metered) street parking.

Coral Gables Map on p132

Top Sight 📷
Fairchild Tropical Garden

The Fairchild is one of America's great tropical botanical gardens. A butterfly grove, tropical plant conservatory and gentle vistas of marsh and keys habitats, plus frequent art installations from artists such as Roy Lichtenstein, all contribute to the beauty of this peaceful, 83-acre garden.

◉ MAP P132, G6

✆ 305-667-1651

www.fairchildgarden.org

10901 Old Cutler Rd

adult/child/senior $25/12/18

🕐 10am-4pm

P 🚻

Creating the Garden

The garden was founded in 1936 by business-man and tropical plant aficionado Robert Montgomery, and named for explorer and scientist David Fairchild. Fairchild, along with environmentalist Marjory Stoneman Douglas and landscape architect William Lyman Phillips (who helped design Boston Common), played a pivotal role in the garden's creation. He donated many of the plants, including the large African baobab growing by the gatehouse. He also went on official plant-collecting expeditions for the garden, sailing a Chinese junk around the Indo-nesian archipelago just before the outbreak of World War II.

Wings of the Tropics

At this indoor gallery, hundreds of butterflies flutter freely through the air, the sheen of their wings glinting in the light. One behind-the-scenes highlight is the **Vollmer Metamor-phosis Lab**, where visitors can watch in real time as chrysalises emerge as butterflies. The butterflies are then released into the Wings of the Tropics exhibit several times a day.

Tropical Plant Conservatory

Amid the lushly lined pathways of the Tropical Plant Conservatory and the **Rare Plant House** is a glass sculpture with colorful tendrils unfurl-ing skyward like flickering flames. Created by American artist Dale Chihuly, the *End of Day Tower* sits in a small pond, with African cichlids swimming about the base of the sculpture.

Richard H Simons Rainforest

Though small in size, this exhibit provides a splendid taste of the tropics, with a little stream and waterfalls amid orchids, plus towering trees with lianas (long woody vines) and epiphytes up in the rainforest canopy.

★ Top Tips

o Start your visit by taking the 45-minute narrated tram tour.

o Time your visit to see daily releases of butterflies in the Wings of the Tropics exhibition (mid-morning and mid-afternoon).

o For the most tranquility, go on weekdays when the crowds are thinnest.

o You can score a discount by coming by bike or on public transit ($5 off each adult ticket, $2 off each child's ticket).

✗ Take a Break

Lakeside Cafe (mains $7-16; ◷9:30am-4:30pm) serves sandwiches, salads and desserts in a pretty open-air setting overlooking Pandanus Lake.

Glasshouse Cafe (mains $6-14; ◷9:30am-4:30pm) serves salads, hot-pressed sandwiches and snacks near the Wings of the Tropics exhibit.

Top Sight 📷
Biltmore Hotel

In the most opulent neighborhood of one of the showiest cities in the world, the Biltmore Hotel has a classic beauty that seems impervious to the passage of years. Its Mediterranean-style architecture, striking interiors and lush tropical grounds can make visitors feel like they've slipped back in time.

◉ MAP P132, C4
☎ 855-311-6903
www.biltmorehotel.com
1200 Anastasia Ave
🅿

The Layout

This opulent hotel spreads across 150 acres that encompass pretty tropical grounds, tennis courts, a massive swimming pool and a restored 18-hole golf course. Inside, there's even more afoot, and indeed, you could spend a few days ensconced in the many activities on offer. The hotel even has its own theater company. GableStage (p139) puts on thought-provoking contemporary works, staged at one end of the Biltmore. It's an intimate theater and there's not a bad seat in the house.

The Design

There's nothing subtle about the soaring central tower, which was modeled after the 12th-century Giralda tower in Seville, Spain. The showy grandeur continues inside, starting with the colonnaded lobby with its hand-painted ceiling, antique chandeliers and Corinthian columns, and continues to the lushly landscaped courtyard set around a central fountain. Back in the day, gondolas transported celebrity guests like Judy Garland and the Vanderbilts around because, of course, there was a private canal system out the back. Though the waterways are gone, the lavish pool, still one of the largest in America, remains.

A Storied Past

Developer George Merrick, who created Coral Gables and founded the University of Miami, joined forces with hotelier John McEntee Bowman to create the Biltmore. The building, the tallest in Florida at the time, opened to much fanfare in 1926 and quickly became one of the icons of the roaring '20s. As well as the rich and famous, members of the mob stayed here, including Al Capone. Thomas 'Fatty' Walsh was gunned down by another gangster on the 13th floor. Some say his ghost still roams the hallways.

★ Top Tips

○ The hotel gives free 45-minute guided tours of the property on Sundays at 1:30pm and 2:30pm.

○ Visitors can swim in the pool and use the fitness center by purchasing a $35 day pass.

○ Plan your visit in the morning or afternoon, when the facade seems to glow with a golden light.

○ Book theater tickets online through www.gablestage.org.

✖ Take a Break

Grab lunch or happy-hour drinks at one of the open-air tables of the **Cascade Poolside Restaurant** (mains $15-29; ⏱11:30am-4pm; ✈).

For something slightly fancier, you can dine on Italian fare at the courtyard restaurant of Fontana (p138).

Coral Gables

E
F
G
H

Alhambra Cir
N Greenway Dr

SW 44th Ave

Hernando St (SW 43rd Ave)

SW 42nd Ave (Le Jeune Rd)

Alcazar Ave

Alhambra Cir

Coral Gables Museum 7

8 ⊗
Giralda Ave
⊗ 10
Aragon Ave

1

14 ⊗
18 ✪ 21
20 🔒

Coral Way

SW 22nd St (Miracle Mile)

Coral Gables City Hall 4 ◉
◉ Coral Gables City Hall

✪ 19 16 🔒

Biltmore Way

Andalusia Ave
11 ⊗
Valencia Ave

12 ⊗ 9 ⊗

2

Galiano St

Cardena St

Valencia Ave
Almeria Ave
Sevilla Ave

Almeria Ave

Palermo Ave

Catalonia Ave

Malaga Ave

Santander Ave

Salzedo St

Ponce Circle Park

Catalonia Ave

3

Anderson Rd

Segovia St

Anastasia Ave

Riviera Dr

University Dr

Sarto Ave

Camilo Ave

Ponce de Leon Blvd

4

Toledo St

CORAL GABLES

Aledo Ave

Cadima Ave

Alesio Ave

Viscaya Ave

Fluvia Ave

Candia Ave

SW 42nd Ave (Le Jeune Rd)

5

Anderson Rd

Palmetto St

University Dr

Hardano St

SW 40th St (Bird Rd)

Ponce de Leon Blvd

2
◉

For reviews see

◉	Top Sights	p128
◉	Sights	p134
⊗	Eating	p136
🍷	Drinking	p138
✪	Entertainment	p139
🔒	Shopping	p139

Fairchild Tropical Garden
◉
3
◉ 🔒 22

E
F
G
H

1 2 3 4 5 6

Sights

Venetian Pool SWIMMING

1 ◉ MAP P132, D3

One of the few pools listed on the National Register of Historic Places, this is a wonderland of rock caves, cascading waterfalls, a palm-fringed island and Venetian-style moorings. Back in 1923 rock was quarried for one of the most beautiful Miami neighborhoods leaving an ugly gash – cleverly, it was laden with mosaic and tiles, and filled up with water. It looks like a Roman emperor's aquatic playground, an absolute delight. Take a swim and follow in the footsteps of stars like Esther Williams and Johnny 'Tarzan' Weissmuller. (📞305-460-5306; www.coralgables. com/venetian-pool; 2701 De Soto Blvd; adult/child Sep-May $15/10, Jun-Aug $20/15; ⏱11am-6:30pm Mon-Fri, 10am-4:30pm Sat & Sun Jun-Aug, closed Dec-Feb, reduced hr Mar-Apr & Oct-Nov; 👫)

Lowe Art Museum MUSEUM

2 ◉ MAP P132, E6

The Lowe, located on the campus of the University of Miami, has a solid collection of modern art, a lovely permanent collection of Renaissance and Baroque paintings, Western sculpture from the 18th to 20th centuries, and archaeological artifacts, art, and crafts from Asia, Africa, the South Pacific and pre-Columbian America. (📞305-284-3535; www.lowe.miami.edu; 1301 Stanford Dr; adult/child/student

Venetian Pool

MARCO BORGHINI/SHUTTERSTOCK©

Plan Your Visit

The main sights in Coral Gables are out of the town center and it's not practical to do much exploring without a car. Although you can see some of the highlights in one long day, to make the most of it consider overnighting in Coral Gables and seeing it all at a more leisurely pace.

$12.50/free/8; ⊙10am-4pm Tue-Sat, from noon Sun)

Matheson Hammock Park   PARK

3 ⊙ MAP P132, G6

This 630-acre county park is the city's oldest, and one of its most scenic. It offers good swimming for children in an enclosed tidal pool, lots of hungry raccoons, dense mangrove swamps and (pretty rare) alligator-spotting. It's just south of Coral Gables. (✆305-665-5475; www.miamidade.gov/parks/matheson-hammock.asp; 9610 Old Cutler Rd; per car weekday/weekend $5/7; ⊙sunrise-sunset; P[⛵])

Coral Gables City Hall   HISTORIC BUILDING

4 ⊙ MAP P132, G2

It's a little funny to think of the often tedious grind of city council business being conducted in this grand building, which opened in 1928 and, architecturally, suggests romance and power, as opposed to parking ordinances. Check out Denman Fink's *Four Seasons* ceiling painting in the tower, as well as his framed,

untitled painting of the underwater world on the 2nd-floor landing. (405 Biltmore Way; ⊙8am-5pm Mon-Fri)

Coral Gables Congregational Church   CHURCH

5 ⊙ MAP P132, C3

Developer George Merrick's father was a New England Congregational minister, so perhaps that accounts for him donating the land for the city's first church. Built in 1924 as a replica of a church in Costa Rica, the yellow-walled, red-roofed exterior is as far removed from New England as...well, Miami. The interior is graced with a beautiful sanctuary and the grounds are landscaped with stately palms. (✆305-448-7421; www.gablesucc.org; 3010 De Soto Blvd; ⊙hours vary)

Merrick House   HISTORIC BUILDING

6 ⊙ MAP P132, D2

It's fun to imagine this simple homestead, with its little hints of Med-style, as the core of what would eventually become the gaudy Gables. When George Merrick's father purchased this plot, site unseen, for $1100, it was all dirt, rock and guavas. The property is now used for meetings and receptions, and you can tour both the house and its pretty organic garden. The modest family residence looks as it did in 1925, outfitted with family photos, furniture and artwork. (📞305-774-0155; 907 Coral Way; adult/child/senior $5/1/3; ⏱tours 1pm, 2pm & 3pm)

Coral Gables Museum MUSEUM

7 ◉ MAP P132, H1

This museum is a well-plotted introduction to the oddball narrative of the founding and growth of the City Beautiful (Coral Gables). The collection includes historical artifacts and mementos from succeeding generations in this tight-knit, eccentric little village. The main building is the old Gables police and fire station (note the deco-style firemen faces jutting out of the facade); it's a lovely architectural blend of Gables' Mediterranean Revival and Miami Beach's muscular, Depression-moderne style. (📞305-603-8067; www.coralgablesmuseum.org; 285 Aragon Ave; adult/child/student $10/5/8; ⏱10am-6pm Mon-Fri, 11am-5pm Sat, noon-5pm Sun)

Eating

Threefold CAFE $

8 ✖ MAP P132, H1

One of Coral Gables' most talked-about cafes is a buzzing, Aussie-run charmer that serves perfectly pulled espressos (and a good

flat white), along with creative breakfasts and lunch fare. Start the morning with waffles and berry compote, smashed avocado toast topped with feta, or a slow-roasted leg of lamb with fried eggs. (📞305-704-8007; www.threefoldcafe.com; 141 Giralda Ave; mains $10-16; ⏱7:30am-3pm Mon, to 4pm Tue-Fri, 7am-4pm Sat & Sun; 🛜📶)

Frenchie's Diner FRENCH $$

9 ✖ MAP P132, H2

Located on a side street, Frenchie's has a tucked away appeal that is quite, well, French. But if the location is 'French-y,' the restaurant itself is the eating out equivalent of blasting *La Marseillaise*. There are black-and-white checkered floors, a chalkboard menu, old prints and mirrors on the walls, and lots of bistro classics: steamed mussels, escargot, onion soup, *steak frites* and the rest. (📞305-442-4554; www.frenchiesdiner.com; 2618 Galiano St; mains lunch $12-36, dinner $21-36; ⏱11am-3pm & 6-10pm Tue-Fri, 6-10pm Sat)

The Local Craft Food & Drink GASTROPUB $$

10 ✖ MAP P132, H1

Brick walls and wooden furniture set a cozy scene here, all enhanced by a menu that presents upscaled comfort food – think pork belly noodles or fried chicken with Nashville hot sauce (ie, very hot) and gremolata, plus a very respectable burger. There's also a huge beer menu and extensive cocktail list. (☎ 305-648-5687; www.facebook.com/thelocal150; 150 Giralda Ave; mains $17-26; ⊙ 11am-2am Sun-Fri, from 4pm Sat)

Bulla Gastrobar   SPANISH $$

11 ⊗ MAP P132, H2

With a festive crowd chattering away over delicious bites of tapas, this stylish spot has great ambience that evokes the lively eating and drinking dens of Madrid. *Patatas bravas* (spicy potatoes), *huevos* 'bulla' (eggs, *serrano* ham and truffle oil) and Iberian ham croquettes keep the crowds coming throughout the night. (☎ 786-810-6215; www.bullagastrobar.com; 2500 Ponce de Leon Blvd; small plates $7-19; ⊙ noon-10pm Mon & Tue,

to 11pm Wed & Thu, to midnight Fri & Sat, 11am-10pm Sun; 🖋)

Pascal's on Ponce   FRENCH $$$

12 ⊗ MAP P132, H2

They're fighting the good fight here: sea scallops with beef short rib, crispy duck confit with wild mushroom fricasée and other French fine-dining classics set the stage for a night of high-end feasting. Pascal's is a favorite among Coral Gables foodies who appreciate time-tested standards.

The menu and the atmosphere rarely change, and frankly that's not a bad thing. After all, if it ain't broke... (☎ 305-444-2024; 2611 Ponce de Leon Blvd; mains lunch $22-31, dinner $31-45; ⊙ 11:30am-2:30pm Mon-Fri, 6-10pm Mon-Thu, to 11pm Fri & Sat)

Matheson Hammock Park (p135)

Matsuri
JAPANESE $$

13 MAP P132, A5

There are many trendy sushi spots in Miami, but while this strip mall restaurant lacks scene, it is often packed with customers seeking real deal, delicious Japanese cuisine (including quite a few South American Japanese). Spicy *toro* (fatty tuna) and scallions, grilled mackerel with natural salt, and an ocean of raw fish are all *oishii* (delicious). (☎305-663-1615; 5759 Bird Rd; mains $7-22; ⏱11:30am-2:30pm Tue-Fri, 5:30-10pm Sun & Tue-Thu, 5:30-11pm Fri & Sat)

Caffe Abbracci
ITALIAN $$$

14 MAP P132, G1

Perfect moments in Coral Gables come easy. Here's a simple formula: you, a loved one, a muggy Miami evening, some delicious pasta and a glass of red at a sidewalk table at Abbracci – one of the finest Italian restaurants in the Gables. (☎305-441-0700; www.caffe abbracci.com; 318 Aragon Ave; mains $26-47; ⏱11:30am-3:30pm Mon-Fri, 6-11pm Sun-Fri, to midnight Sat)

Fontana
ITALIAN $$$

15 MAP P132, C4

In the handsomely designed courtyard restaurant of the Biltmore Hotel (p130), you can dine on Italian cooking like roasted pumpkin and shrimp ravioli, squid ink and lobster ravioli, and oven-roasted rabbit with braised leeks and mushrooms. (☎305-913-3189; Biltmore Hotel, 1200 Anastasia Ave; mains $17-48; ⏱11:30am-3pm & 6-10pm daily)

Drinking

Copper 29
BAR

16 MAP P132, H2

Portraits of celebrities like Brad Pitt in a Napoleonic military uniform or the Mona Lisa in hipster glasses gaze at a crowd of Coral Gables pretty people throwing back serious cocktails like the La Vie en Rose (tequila, mezcal, blood orange and vanilla foam). There's a dark and sexy speakeasy vibe, although come the weekend the spot becomes more of a dance-y lounge. (☎786-580-4689; http:// copper29bar.com; 206 Miracle Mile; ⏱5pm-1am Mon & Tue, to 2am Wed & Thu, 4pm-2am Fri, noon-2am Sat, to 1am Sun)

Titanic Brewing Company
MICROBREWERY

17 MAP P132, B6

By day Titanic is an all-American-type brewpub, but at night it turns into a popular University of Miami watering hole. Titanic's signature brews are refreshing and there's good pub grub on hand, including Sriracha wings and peel-and-eat shrimp.

It is located by the University entrance near Dixie Hwy and Red Rd (SW 57th Ave). (☎305-668-1742; www.titanicbrewery.com; 5813 Ponce de Leon Blvd; ⏱11:30am-1am Sun-Thu, to 2am Fri & Sat)

Entertainment

Coral Gables Art Cinema
CINEMA

18 ⭐ MAP P132, H1

In the epicenter of Coral Gables' downtown, you'll find one of Miami's best art-house cinemas. It shows indie and foreign films in a modern 144-seat screening room. Check out cult favorites shown in the original 35mm format at Saturday midnight screenings (part of the After Hours series). (📞786-385-9689; www.gablescinema.com; 260 Aragon Ave)

GableStage
THEATER

Founded as the Florida Shakespeare Theatre in 1979 and now housed on the property of the Biltmore Hotel (see 👁 Map p132, C4) in Coral Gables, this company still performs an occasional Shakespeare play, but mostly presents contemporary and classical pieces. (📞305-445-1119; www.gablestage.org; 1200 Anastasia Ave)

Actors' Playhouse
THEATER

19 ⭐ MAP P132, G2

Housed within the 1948 deco Miracle Theater in Coral Gables, this three-theater venue stages musicals and comedies, children's theater on its kids stage and more avant-garde productions in its small experimental black-box space. (📞305-444-9293; www.actorsplayhouse.org; Miracle Theater, 280 Miracle Mile; tickets $20-65)

Shopping

Retro City Collectibles
MUSIC

20 🔒 MAP P132, H2

This cluttered little upstairs den of geekery is a fun place to browse, with all manner of eye-catching and collectible genre artifacts. You'll find comic books, records, baseball cards, Pez dispensers, old film posters and action figures (*Star Wars*, *Star Trek*, *Dr Who* etc). (Gables Records n Comics; 📞786-879-4407; 277 Miracle Mile, 2nd fl; ⏰3-6pm Wed-Fri, 1-7pm Sat, to 4pm Sun)

Books & Books
BOOKS

21 🔒 MAP P132, H1

The best indie bookstore in South Florida is a wonderful place to stock up on your beach reading material and see authors in action at one of the frequent in-store events. There's a nice cafe and restaurant, with dining on a Mediterranean-like patio fronting the shop. (📞305-442-4408; https://booksandbooks.com; 265 Aragon Ave; ⏰9am-11pm Sun-Thu, to midnight Fri & Sat)

Boy Meets Girl
CHILDREN'S CLOTHING

22 🔒 MAP P132, G6

Fantastically upscale and frankly expensive clothing for wee ones – if the kids are getting past puberty, look elsewhere, but otherwise they'll be fashionable far before they realize it. (📞305-445-9668; www.bmgkids.com; 358 San Lorenzo Ave, Village of Merrick Park; ⏰10am-8pm Mon-Sat, 11am-7pm Sun)

Worth a Trip 🔭
Everglades National Park

There is no wilderness in America quite like the Everglades. Called the 'River of Grass' by Native American inhabitants, this is not just a wetland, or a swamp, or a lake, or a river, or a prairie, or a grassland – it is all of those, twisted together into a series of soft horizons, long vistas, and near-mystical wildlife encounters.

📞 305-242-7700

www.nps.gov/ever

40001 State Rd 9336, Homestead

vehicle pass $30, pedestrian & cyclist $15

🕑 visitor center 9am-5pm

Wildlife

The Everglades provide rich habitat for a wide range of animals. These include over 40 species of mammals, 50 different reptiles, 300 fish species, 700 different plants and more then 360 bird species.

Alligators are the most commonly seen large animal in the park, although not so much in the 10,000 Islands, as they tend to avoid saltwater. They are considered a keystone species in the Everglades, where they play an important role in the ecosystem – alligator dens, for example, are often used later by numerous other species. Although plentiful now with more than 200,000 thought to inhabit the Everglades (and a Florida-wide population of around 1.5 million)

If you're traveling along the coastal sections of the Everglades, including the 10,000 Islands, watch for bottlenose dolphins. Beautiful, streamlined creatures, they usually measure 10ft to 14ft in length and have smooth gray skin.

Another charismatic Everglades presence, the playful river otter is sometimes known as the 'playboy of the Everglades.' The river otter is rarely out of the water during daylight hours. Their webbed feet, sleek design and powerful jaws combine to make them swift swimmers and excellent hunters of turtles, fish and even baby alligators.

Kayaking & Canoeing

The waterways of the Everglades rank among the best kayaking destinations anywhere in the US – there are infinite trails, plenty of wildlife to keep you company, and numerous highly professional operators to get you out on the water.

In the Northern Everglades, paddlers have seemingly endless choice, with countless Everglades channels to choose from and the 10,000 Islands just offshore.

★ Top Tips

○ Dry season (December to March) is the best time for seeing wildlife, but some kayaking watercourses may be tough to access. April to June has a mix of water and wildlife.

○ Do not feed the alligators; it is both illegal and dangerous.

○ The 'Glades are flat, which makes them good for bicycling, but beware narrow road shoulders.

✖ Take a Break

Have a screamingly fresh fruit smoothie at the wonderful **Robert Is Here** (📞 305-246-1592; www.robertishere.com; 19200 SW 344th St, Homestead; juices $7-10; ⏰ 8am-7pm).

Swamp-shack venues don't get much more atmospheric than **Joanie's Blue Crab Café** (📞 239-695-2682; www.joaniesbluecrabcafe.com; 39395 Tamiami Trail E; mains $8-17; ⏰ 11am-5pm Thu-Tue; closed seasonally, call to confirm; 🅿️).

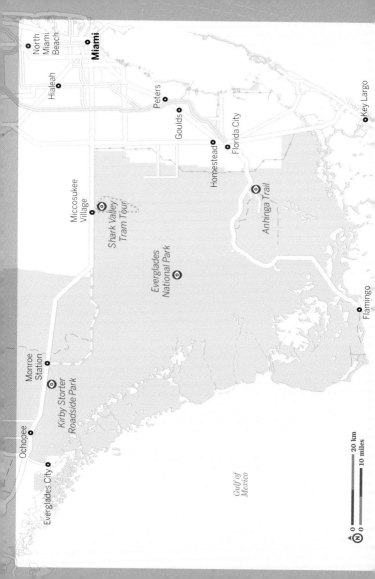

North Miami Beach

Miami

Hialeah

Peters

Goulds

Homestead

Florida City

Key Largo

Miccosukee Village

Shark Valley Tram Tour

Anhinga Trail

Everglades National Park

Flamingo

Monroe Station

Kirby Storter Roadside Park

Ochopee

Everglades City

Gulf of Mexico

N

0   20 km
0   10 miles

Wilderness Waterway (99 miles)

This route between Everglades City and Flamingo, is the longest canoe trail in the area. Most islands are fringed by narrow beaches with sugar-white sand, but note that the water is brackish and very shallow most of the time. It's not Tahiti, but it's fascinating. You can camp on your own island for up to a week.

The highly recommended **Everglades Adventures** (📞 877-567-0679; https://iveyhouse.com/everglades-adventures; 107 Camellia St, Everglades City; 3-4hr tours adult/child from $99/59, canoe/kayak rental per day from $45/55) offers a range of half-day kayak tours, from sunrise paddles to twilight trips through mangroves that return under a sky full of stars. Tours shuttle you to places like Chokoloskee Island, Collier-Seminole State Park, Rabbit Key or Tiger Key for excursions. Everglades Adventures also provides a one-way shuttle service (from Flamingo back to Everglades City) for those making the seven- to 10-day trip along the Wilderness Waterway.

In the Southern Everglades, the real joy is canoeing into the bracken heart of the swamp. There are plenty of push-off points, all with names that sound like they were read off Frodo's map to Mordor, including **Hell's Bay**, the **Nightmare**, **Snake Bight** and **Graveyard Creek**.

Nine Mile Pond (3 or 5.2 mile loop)

Paddle through grassy marshes and mangrove islands, following the numbered white poles; for the shorter version, take the cut-through from marker #44. Allow four hours for the full loop. It's good for alligators, wading birds and turtles.

Hell's Bay (5.5 miles one way)

Despite the frightening name (and terrible mosquitoes), this can be a magnificent place to kayak. 'Hell to get into and hell to get out of' was how this sheltered launch was described by old Gladesmen, but once inside you'll find a capillary network of mangrove creeks, sawgrass islands and shifting mudflats, where the brambles form a green tunnel and all you can smell is sea salt and the dark organic breath of the swamp. Allow six to eight hours for the return trip.

On the property of the Robert Is Here (p141) fruit stand, **Garls Coastal Kayaking Everglades** (📞 305-393-3223; www.garlscoastalkayaking.com; 19200 SW 344th St, Homestead; single/double kayak per day $40/55, half-/full-day tour $125/160) leads highly recommended excursions into the Everglades. A full-day 'Day in the Glades' outing includes hiking (more of a wet walk or slog into the lush landscape of cypress domes), followed by kayaking in both the mangroves and in Florida Bay, and, time permitting, a night walk. For a DIY adventure, you can also hire kayaks as well as other equipment – including tents, sleeping bags and fishing gear.

Hiking

Getting out on the water may allow you to go deeper into the Everglades wilderness, but the numerous hiking trails are more accessible, even to those with very basic levels of fitness. Most trails are no longer than one-mile return, although there are a couple of longer trails to really leave behind the crowds.

In the Northern Everglades, some standout trails include the following:

Kirby Storter Roadside Park (1 mile return) Probably the pick of the short walks close to the main road. Though short in terms of length, this elevated **boardwalk** (www.nps.gov/bicy/planyourvisit/kirby -storter-roadside-park.htm) leads to a lovely overlook where you can often see a variety of birdlife (ibis and red-shouldered hawks) amid tall cypresses and strangler figs, plus of course alligators.

Bobcat Boardwalk Trail (0.5-mile loop) At the park entrance going into Shark Valley, this easy trail makes a loop through a thick copse of tropical hardwoods before emptying you out right back into the Shark Valley parking lot.

Otter Cave Trail (0.25 miles one-way) In a similar area, this trail heads over a limestone shelf that has been Swiss-cheesed into a porous sponge by rainwater. Animals now live in the eroded holes (although it's not likely you'll spot any) and Native Americans used to live on top of the shelf.

Shark Valley Trail (15 miles return) This excellent trail takes you past small creeks, tropical forest

Kayaking through the mangroves, Everglades National Park

and 'borrow pits' (human-made holes that are now basking spots for gators, turtles and birdlife). The pancake-flat trail is perfect for bicycles, which can be rented at the entrance for $10 per hour. Bring water with you. If you don't feel like exerting yourself, the most popular and painless way to immerse yourself in the Everglades is via the two-hour **tram tour** (305-221-8455; www.sharkvalleytramtours.com; adult/child under 12yr/senior $27/21/14; departures 9:30am, 11am, 2pm & 4pm May-Dec, 9am-4pm Jan-Apr hourly on the hour) that runs along Shark Valley's entire 15-mile trail.

In the Southern Everglades, our pick of the trail mix includes the following:

Anhinga Trail (0.8 mile one way) This is *the* trail you shouldn't miss in the Everglades. You'll get a close-up view of gators and birds on this short trail that begins at the **Royal Palm Visitor Center** (305-242-7237; www.nps.gov/ever/planyourvisit/royal-palm.htm; State Rd 9336; 9am-4:15pm); you can sometimes see dozens of alligators piled together in the day. The park also offers periodic ranger-led walks along the boardwalk at night, though you can always do this by yourself.

West Lake Trail (1.8 miles one way) This trail runs through the largest protected mangrove forest in the northern hemisphere.

Christian Point (2 miles one way) This dramatic walk takes you under tropical forest, past columns of white cypress and over a series of mudflats, and ends with a dramatic view of the windswept shores of Florida Bay.

Bear Lake (1.6 miles one way) Hardwood hammock and mangroves line the Homestead Canal along a trail rich in woodland birds and Caribbean tree species. You can drive to the trailhead from the main road; otherwise, add 2 miles to the walk one way.

Coastal Prairie Trail (7.5 miles one way) Follow the traditional path of fishermen across open prairies and stands of button-woods. It begins at the **Flamingo Campground** (www.nps.gov/ever/planyourvisit/flamdirections.htm); a shorter version off the main trail and called **Bayshore Loop (2-mile loop)** is an alternative for those with limited time.

Survival Guide

Cuban restaurant, Little Havana KAMIRA/SHUTTERSTOCK ©

Before You Go

Book Your Stay

Miami has some of the finest hotels in the world – lodging options that balance cutting-edge design with first-rate amenities. South Beach has its boutique beauties and Coral Gables has its historic charmers, while Downtown is famed for high-rises with sweeping views and endless amenities, and mid-century modern – MiMo – 'motels' along Biscayne Boulevard.

Useful Websites

Greater Miami & the Beaches (www. miamiandbeaches.com/ where-to-stay) Lowdown on great stays in Miami, whether you're after luxury, architectural beauty or ocean views.

Lonely Planet (www. lonelyplanet.com/usa/ miami/hotels) Accommodation reviews and online booking services.

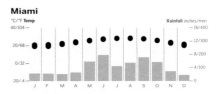

Miami
°C/°F Temp
40/104 ─

20/68 ─

0/32 ─

-20/-4 ─
                J F M A M J J A S O N D

Rainfall inches/mm
─ 16/400

─ 12/300

─ 8/200

─ 4/100

─ 0

When to Go

○ **Winter (Dec–Feb)**
The warm, dry weather draws tourists; hotel prices and crowds are at their peak, though it's also the liveliest season with a packed calendar of festivals and events.

○ **Spring (Mar–Jun)**
Not as muggy as deep summer, but lusher and greener than winter.

○ **Summer (Jul–Sep)** It's hot! Prices plummet. When the temperatures aren't sweltering there are storms: it's hurricane season.

○ **Autumn (Oct–Nov)**
Shoulder season can yield decent prices, while the warm weather ensures ample beach days.

Best Budget

New Yorker (www. hotelnewyorkermiami. com) At the top of the budget category, but undeniably cool (check the patio bar!).

SoBe Hostel (www.sobe -hostel.com) Great South Beach location with a friendly crowd and lots of activities.

Extended Stay (www. extendedstayamerica.com) A nicely executed chain hotel with good Coral Gables pedestrian access.

Best Midrange

Vagabond Hotel (www. thevagabondhotelmiami. com) Restored 1950s beauty, with retro rooms and a lovely pool bar.

Freehand Miami (www. thefreehand.com) Affordable dorms, stylish private rooms and a beautiful backyard.

Eurostars Langford (www.eurostarshotels. co.uk) Classy Downtown option in a beaux-arts beauty.

Palihouse Miami Beach (www.palisociety.

com/hotels/miami-beach)
A brilliant blend of deco design and Mediterranean good looks.

Best Top End

Washington Park Hotel (www.wphsouth beach.com) A hotel spread among five deco buildings with an eye-catching courtyard pool and a great bar.

Betsy Hotel (www. thebetsyhotel.com) South Beach choice for excellent service and literary scenesters.

1 Hotel (www.1hotels. com/south-beach) Green credentials, multiple pools, a kids club and rooms that you'll never want to leave.

Faena Hotel Miami Beach (www.faena. com/miami-beach) Lush grounds, decadent rooms, and butler service to boot.

Setai (www.thesetaihotel. com) Cross a Balinese temple with a deco hotel, then throw in countless amenities.

Biltmore Hotel (www. biltmorehotel.com) Gem of Mediterranean Revival style, amenities galore – including Florida's biggest pool.

Arriving in Miami

Miami International Airport

Located 6 miles west of Downtown, the busy **Miami International Airport** (MIA; ☎ 305-876-7000; www.miami-airport. com; 2100 NW 42nd Ave) has three terminals and serves more than 45 million passengers each year. There are left-luggage facilities at Concourse E in the Central Terminal (call ☎ 305-869-1163 for more information).

Fort Lauderdale-Hollywood International Airport

Fort Lauderdale-Hollywood International Airport (www.fll. net), around 26 miles north of Downtown Miami, largely serves domestic passengers and is well connected to major hubs such as New York and Atlanta.

Port of Miami

The **Port of Miami** (☎ 305-347-4800; www. miamidade.gov/portmiami) receives around five million passengers each year. Arriving in the port will put you on the edge of Downtown Miami; taxis and public buses to other points are available on nearby Biscayne Blvd.

Getting Around

Car

○ You must pay for parking nearly everywhere (though it's generally free from 3am to 8am – from midnight in some places). If you park without paying, you may be towed and have to pay upwards of $200 (plus the headache!) to retrieve your vehicle.

○ Most on-street parking is now done by smartphone app or pay by phone (though there are still a few pay-and-display ticket machines at some locations). The app to use in Miami is Pay By Phone (www. paybyphone.com). In

Miami Beach, you'll need to use Park Mobile (www.parkmobile.com).

○ Parking rates vary, but typically range between $1.50 and $3 per hour. There are many municipal parking garages, which are usually the easiest and cheapest option – look for giant blue 'P' signs. You'll find several located along Collins Ave and Washington Ave in South Beach.

Taxi & Ride-Sharing

○ For a 20-minute trip (Lincoln Rd to Brickell City Center, for instance), the fare is upwards of $30.

○ Given the high prices of taxis, and inconvenience of ordering them, most Miami residents use ride-sharing apps such as Lyft and Uber.

○ Taxis are hard to hail on the street. You'll generally have to call one.

○ **Central Cab** (☎305-532-5555) is one of the big taxi operators.

Bus

○ Miami's local bus system is called **Metrobus** (☎305-891-3131; www.

miamidade.gov/transit/routes.asp; tickets $2.25) and, though it has an extensive route system, service can be slow.

○ Each bus route has a different schedule and routes generally run from about 5:30am to 11pm, though some are 24 hours.

○ Rides cost $2.25 and must be paid in exact change (coins or a combination of bills and coins) or with an Easy Card (available for purchase from Metrorail stations and some shops and pharmacies).

○ An easy-to-read route map is available online. Note that if you have to transfer buses, you'll have to pay the fare each time if paying in cash. With an Easy Card, transfers are free.

Trolley

○ A free bus service runs along routes in Miami, Miami Beach, Coconut Grove, Little Havana and Coral Gables, among other locations. The Trolley (www.miamigov.com/trolley) is actually a hybrid-electric bus disguised as an orange and green trolley.

○ Miami Beach (www.miamibeachfl.gov/transportation) has four trolleys running along different routes, with arrivals every 10 to 15 minutes from 8am to midnight (from 6am Monday to Saturday on some routes).

Bicycle

○ Miami is flat, but traffic can be horrendous (abundant and fast-moving), and there isn't much of a biking culture (or respect for bikers) just yet.

○ **Citi Bike** (☎305-532-9494; www.citibikemiami.com; rental per 30min $4.50, 1/2/4hr $6.50/10/18, day $24) is a bike-share program where you can borrow a bike from scores of kiosks spread around Miami and Miami Beach.

○ For longer rides, clunky Citi Bikes are not ideal (no helmet, no lock and only three gears). Instead, hire a bike from **Bike & Roll** (☎305-604-0001; www.bikemiami.com; 210 10th St; rental per 2/4hr from $15/20, per day from $25, tours $49; ⏰9am-7pm) or **Brickell Bikes** (☎305-373-3633; www.brickellbikes.com; 70 SW

12th St; bike hire per 4/9hr from $20/25; ⊙10am-7pm Mon-Fri, to 6pm Sat).

Essential Information

Accessible Travel

Most public buildings are wheelchair accessible and have appropriate restroom facilities. Transportation services are generally accessible to all, and telephone companies provide relay operators for the hearing impaired. Many banks provide ATM instructions in Braille, curb ramps are common and many busy intersections have audible crossing signals.

There are a number of organizations that specialize in the needs of disabled travelers.

Miami & the Beaches (www.miamiandbeaches. com/plan-your-trip/ accessible-travel) Accessible travel information specific to the Miami area.

Mobility International USA (www.miusa.org) Advises disabled travelers on mobility issues and runs an educational exchange program.

For more information, download Lonely Planet's free *Accessible Travel* guide from http://lptravel.to/ AccessibleTravel.

Business Hours

Unless otherwise noted the standard business hours in Miami are as follows:

Banks 8:30am to 4:30pm Monday to Thursday, to 5:30pm Friday; sometimes 9am to 12:30pm Saturday.

Bars In Miami, most bars open 5pm to 3am; in Miami Beach, most bars close at 5am.

Businesses 9am to 7pm Monday to Friday.

Restaurants Breakfast 7am to 10:30am Monday to Friday; brunch 9am to 2pm Saturday and Sunday; lunch 11:30am to 2:30pm Monday to Friday; dinner 5pm to 10pm, later Friday and Saturday.

Post Offices 9am to 5pm Monday to Friday; sometimes to noon Saturday.

Shops 10am to 6pm Monday to Saturday, noon to 5pm Sunday; shopping malls keep extended hours.

Electricity

Type A
120V/60Hz

Type B
120V/60Hz

Emergencies

Ambulance, Police, Fire ☏911

Beach Patrol ☏305-673-7714

Hurricane Hotline ☏305-468-5400

Health

The United States offers excellent health care. The problem is it can be prohibitively expensive. It's essential to purchase travel-health insurance if your policy doesn't cover you when you're abroad.

If your health insurance does not cover you for medical expenses abroad, consider obtaining supplemental health or travel insurance. Find out in advance whether your insurance plan will make payments directly to the providers or if it will reimburse you later for any overseas health expenditures.

We have to stress: a simple visit to the doctor's office can cost hundreds of dollars, and a hospital stay will cost thousands if you aren't covered by insurance.

Medical Services

Coral Gables Hospital (☏866-661-3359, emergency room 305-445-8461; www.coralgableshospital.com; 3100 Douglas Rd, Coral Gables) A community-based facility with many bilingual doctors.

CVS Pharmacy Pharmacy chain has many locations, including one in **South Beach** (☏305-538-1571; 1421 Alton Rd, South Beach; ⊗7am-9pm).

Miami Beach Community Health Center (Stanley C Meyers Center; ☏305-538-8835; www.mbchc.org; 710 Alton Rd, South Beach; ⊗7am-5pm Mon-Fri) Walk-in clinic with long lines.

Mount Sinai Medical Center (☏305-676-6496, emergency room 305-563-8026; www.msmc.com; 4300 Alton Rd; ⊗24hr) The area's best emergency room. Be aware that you must eventually pay, and fees are high.

Legal Matters

○ If you are stopped by the police, there is no system for paying traffic tickets or other fines on the spot. The patrol officer will explain your options to you; there is usually a 30-day period to pay fines by mail.

○ Medical marijuana is legal in Florida, but possession of more than 20 grams or any other controlled substance is a felony and can lead to your arrest. You are not allowed to smoke marijuana in public on Miami Beach.

○ If you're arrested, you are allowed to remain silent, though never walk away from an officer. You are entitled to have access to an attorney. The legal system presumes you're innocent until proven guilty.

○ All persons who are arrested have the right to make one phone call. If you don't have a lawyer or family member to help you, call your embassy or consulate. The police will give you the number on request.

Media

○ **Newspapers**
The *Miami Herald* (www.miamiherald.com) is the major daily covering local, national and international news, and

El Nuevo Herald (www.el nuevoherald.com) is its Spanish-language edition. *Diario Las Américas* (www.diariolasameri cas.com) is another Spanish-language daily. *Miami New Times* (www. miaminewtimes.com) is a free alternative weekly paper. *Sun-Sentinel* (www.sun-sentinel.com) is a daily covering South Florida.

○ **Radio** WLRN (www. wlrn.org) is the local National Public Radio affiliate, at 91.3FM on the dial.

Money

ATMs are widely available, though most ATM withdrawals using out-of-state cards incur surcharges of $3 or so. Major credit cards are widely accepted.

Public Holidays

On the following national public holidays, banks, schools and government offices (including post offices) are closed, and transportation, museums and other services operate on a Sunday schedule. Many stores, however, maintain regular business

hours. Holidays falling on a weekend are usually observed the following Monday.

New Year's Day January 1

Martin Luther King Jr Day Third Monday in January

Presidents Day Third Monday in February

Memorial Day Last Monday in May

Independence Day July 4

Labor Day First Monday in September

Columbus Day Second Monday in October

Veterans Day November 11

Thanksgiving Fourth Thursday in November

Christmas Day December 25

Safe Travel

Miami is a big city with big city crime issues. A few areas are considered by locals to be dangerous:

○ Liberty City, in northwest Miami; Overtown, from 14th to 20th Sts; Little Haiti and stretches of the Miami riverfront.

○ The western edges of Downtown can feel lonely at night.

In these and other reputedly unsafe areas you should avoid walking around alone late at night. It's best to take a taxi or ride share.

○ Be vigilant of drink spiking and other date rape activities in bars and clubs.

○ Hurricanes are no joke, and cause the city to shut down.

Environmental Dangers

○ Natural dangers include the strong sun (use a high-SPF sunscreen) and mosquitoes (use a spray-on repellent).

○ Hurricane season is between June and November. There's a hurricane hotline (☎305-468-5400), which will give you information about approaching storms, storm tracks, warnings and estimated time to touchdown – all the things you will need to know to make a decision about if and when to leave.

Time

Miami is in the US eastern time zone:

Miami Tips

o **Languages** If you're darker skinned, expect many locals to initially speak to you in Spanish (even though many Miami Spanish speakers are blonde and blue-eyed). If you don't speak Spanish, politely say, '*lo siento, no hablo español*' ('sorry, I don't speak Spanish').

o **Don't drive during rush hour** From 7am to 9am and 4pm to 6pm, the roads of Miami are *packed*. It can take hours to drive across even a few neighborhoods at this time.

noon in Miami equals 9am in San Francisco and 5pm in London. During daylight-saving time, clocks move forward one hour in March and move back one hour in November.

Toilets

You'll find public toilets at some parks and at various posts along city beaches. Outside of these locations, public toilets can be sparse.

Tourist Information

Greater Miami & the Beaches Convention & Visitors Bureau

(📞 305-539-3000; www.miamiandbeaches.com; 701 Brickell Ave, 27th fl; ⏰ 8:30am-6pm Mon-Fri) Offers loads of info on Miami and keeps up-to-date with the latest events and cultural offerings.

Visas

o All visitors should reconfirm entry requirements and visa guidelines before arriving.

o You can get visa information through www.usa.gov, but the US State Department (www.travel.state.gov) maintains the most comprehensive visa information, with lists of consulates

and downloadable application forms.

o The Visa Waiver Program allows citizens of three dozen countries to enter the USA for stays of 90 days or less without first obtaining a US visa. See the ESTA website (https://esta.cbp.dhs.gov) for a current list. Under this program you must have a nonrefundable return ticket and 'e-passport' with digital chip.

o Visitors who don't qualify for the Visa Waiver Program need a visa. Basic requirements are a valid passport, recent photo, travel details and often proof of financial stability.

o To stay longer than the date stamped on your passport, visit a local USCIS (www.uscis.gov) office.

Behind the Scenes

Send Us Your Feedback

We love to hear from travelers – your comments help make our books better. We read every word, and we guarantee that your feedback goes straight to the authors. Visit **lonelyplanet.com/contact** to submit your updates and suggestions.

Note: We may edit, reproduce and incorporate your comments in Lonely Planet products such as guidebooks, websites and digital products, so let us know if you don't want your comments reproduced or your name acknowledged. For a copy of our privacy policy visit lonelyplanet.com/privacy.

Adam's Thanks

Thank you: Victoria Smith, Anthony Ham, Regis St Louis, and the rest of the Florida team; Chris Romaguera, for rum, recommendations, and brotherhood; mom and dad for bringing me here; Rachel, Sanda and Isaac for being with me. *Por ti, mami.*

Anthony's Thanks

Thanks to Luke Hunter, Tim Tetzlaff, Mark Lotz, Lisa and David Korte and others for their invaluable help. Thanks to the wonderful Vicky Smith, everyone at Lonely Planet for getting this book out there at an extremely difficult time. Thanks to Jan for always being the faithful follower of my journeys. And to Marina, Carlota and Valentina: *os he echado mucho de menos y os quiero.*

Acknowledgements

Cover photograph: Ocean Drive, Miami Beach, Sean Pavone/ Shutterstock ©
Photographs pp30-1 (from left): Meuniers; ImageMD; Miami2You/ Shutterstock ©

This Book

This 2nd edition of Lonely Planet's *Pocket Miami* guidebook was researched and written by Adam Karlin and Anthony Ham. The previous edition was researched and written by Regis St Louis. This guidebook was produced by the following:

Senior Product Editors Daniel Bolger, Victoria Smith

Regional Senior Cartographers Alison Lyall, Hunor Csutoros

Coordinating Editor Lorna Parkes

Product Editor Martine Power

Book Designer Michael Weldon

Assisting Editors Sasha Drew, Kate James

Cover Researcher Brendan Dempsey-Spencer

Thanks to Laura Roy Daniel, Karen Henderson, Sandie Kestell, Amy Lysen, Genna Patterson, Angela Tinson

Index

See also separate subindexes for:

✪ **Eating p158**

○ **Drinking p159**

✪ **Entertainment p159**

○ **Shopping p159**

Our Writers

Adam Karlin

Miami Adam has contributed to dozens of Lonely Planet guidebooks, covering an alphabetical spread that ranges from the Andaman Islands to the Zimbabwe Border. As a journalist, he has written on travel, crime, politics, archeology, and the Sri Lankan Civil War, among other topics. He has sent dispatches from every continent barring Antarctica (one day!) and his essays and articles have featured in the BBC, NPR, and multiple nonfiction anthologies.

Anthony Ham

Everglades National Park Anthony is a freelance writer who travels the world in search of stories. His particular passions are the wildlife, wild places and wide open spaces of the planet, from the Great Plains of the US to the Amazon, East and Southern Africa, and the Arctic. He writes for magazines and newspapers around the world, and his narrative nonfiction book on Africa's lions was published in 2020. An Australian, Anthony divides his time between Melbourne and Madrid (where he lived for 10 years).

Published by Lonely Planet Global Limited
CRN 554153
2nd edition – Jun 2021
ISBN 978 1 78701 743 6
© Lonely Planet 2021 Photographs © as indicated 2021
10 9 8 7 6 5 4 3 2 1
Printed in Malaysia